Advance Praise

The book is informative and focuses on fundamentals of venture capital investments. It is easy to follow and helps grasp basic and practical concepts about venture capital investments.

—**Pankaj Singal,** Vice President,
Head of Data Governance, Marcus by Goldman Sachs, NY

The authors have written a prolific piece on the Indian venture capital market that will help students, academicians, practitioners alike. It helps understand this nascent and burgeoning segment with extensive examples. It approaches the venture business holistically and has cradle to grave coverage of the entire deal life cycle including the fund business. A must read!

—**Puneet Gupta,** Managing Director,
Kentrus Investment Advisors Private Limited

What I liked in *Venture Capital Investments* is the flow of the chapters. Each chapter seamlessly and logically flows into the next and ensures that a reader (technical or non-technical) understands the concepts completely. After my previous company exit and in my current company (funded by leading venture capitalists), this was a refreshing read and allowed me to brush-up my concepts!

—**Visham Sikand,** Founder and Managing Director,
Goals101 Data Solutions

This book will provide an opportunity for inventors and innovators to motivate and expand the scope of start-up businesses in India and other emerging economies. As a primer, the contents are digestible to readers having no previous background in business management, start-up or otherwise. I would strongly recommend the book to science, technology, engineering and mathematics (STEM) practitioners.

—**Mike Vinson,** President and Chief Operating Officer,
Averatek Corporation

venture
capital
investments

The *SAGE Essentials* series aims to arm professionals with bite-sized learning on technical and relevant topics, helping them to stay ahead in the knowledge-powered economy. It offers a range of pithy books on topics of current interest for business and management professionals. Books in the series, authored by subject matter experts, provide a historically entrenched preamble to the subject, following it up with invaluable insights, practical ideas and future trends. In a volatile and rapidly changing business and technological environment, these short and succinct books aim to help professionals from diverse backgrounds and industries upskill by broadening their knowledge and enhancing their learning capacities.

SAGE ESSENTIALS

venture
capital
investments

Raj Kumar
Manu Sharma

Los Angeles | London | New Delhi
Singapore | Washington DC | Melbourne

S A G E   E S S E N T I A L S

First published in 2020 by

SAGE Publications India Pvt Ltd
B1/I-1 Mohan Cooperative Industrial Area
Mathura Road, New Delhi 110 044, India
www.sagepub.in

SAGE Publications Inc
2455 Teller Road
Thousand Oaks, California 91320, USA

SAGE Publications Ltd
1 Oliver's Yard, 55 City Road
London EC1Y 1SP, United Kingdom

SAGE Publications Asia-Pacific Pte Ltd
18 Cross Street #10-10/11/12
China Square Central
Singapore 048423

Published by Vivek Mehra for SAGE Publications India Pvt Ltd. Typeset in 9/13.5 pt Georgia by AG Infographics, Delhi.

Library of Congress Cataloging-in-Publication Data

Names: Kumar, Raj, 1959- author. | Sharma, Manu (Financial researcher), author.
Title: Venture capital investments / Raj Kumar, Manu Sharma.
Description: Thousand Oaks : SAGE Publishing, 2020. | Series: Sage essentials | Includes
    bibliographical references.
Identifiers: LCCN 2020014965 | ISBN 9789353884154 (paperback) | ISBN 9789353884161
    (epub) | ISBN 9789353884178 (ebook)
Subjects: LCSH: Venture capital. | Capital investments.
Classification: LCC HG4751 .K86 2020 | DDC 332/.04154—dc23
LC record available at https://lccn.loc.gov/2020014965

ISBN: 978-93-5388-415-4 (PB)

SAGE Team: Namarita Kathait, Shruti Gupta and Aishna Bhatt

Dedication

To the readers who are interested in gaining fundamental knowledge of venture capital investments and working of venture capital industry in India.

Thank you for choosing a SAGE product!
If you have any comment, observation or feedback,
I would like to personally hear from you.

Please write to me at **contactceo@sagepub.in**

Vivek Mehra, Managing Director and CEO, SAGE India.

Bulk Sales

SAGE India offers special discounts
for purchase of books in bulk.
We also make available special imprints
and excerpts from our books on demand.

For orders and enquiries, write to us at

Marketing Department
SAGE Publications India Pvt Ltd
B1/I-1, Mohan Cooperative Industrial Area
Mathura Road, Post Bag 7
New Delhi 110044, India

E-mail us at **marketing@sagepub.in**

Subscribe to our mailing list
Write to **marketing@sagepub.in**

This book is also available as an e-book.

Contents

Contents

List of Abbreviations

BSE	Bombay Stock Exchange
CAPM	Capital Asset Pricing Model
D&A	Depreciation and amortization
EBIT	Earnings before interest and taxes
EBITDA	Earnings before interest, tax, depreciation and amortization
EM	Exit multiple
EV	Enterprise value
FCFF	Free cash flows to the firm
GP	General partner
IPO	Initial public offering
LP	Limited partner
MVE	Market value of equity
NI	Net income
P/E	Price-to-earnings
R_m	Revenue multiple
VC	Venture capital
WACC	Weighted Average Cost of Capital

Acknowledgements

I would like to thank my parents, wife and children for their continued support. Without the support of my wife and children and blessing of my parents, it would not have been possible for me to take time to write the book. I would like to thank Mr Puneet Gupta (MD, Kentrus Investment Advisors Private Limited) for discussions on deal evaluation, venture economics and venture structure. I would also like to thank Shalini Singh and Manisha Mathews of SAGE for their extended help and support in the publication of this book. Most importantly, I would like to thank Namarita Kathait of SAGE for reading the initial drafts and advising on improving the quality of write-ups.

—**Raj Kumar**

I would like to thank my father, Dr Surinder Sharma, for his immense support throughout my life. I would also like to thank my wife, Dr Radhika Sharma, for her support in taking care of our son, Devaansh, while I was away writing this book. Without the support of my wife and blessings of my father, it would not have been possible for me to take time out to write this book. I would like to thank Mr Puneet Gupta (MD, Kentrus Investment Advisors Private Limited) for discussions on deal evaluation, venture economics and venture structure. I would also like to thank Shalini Singh and Manisha Mathews for their extended help and support in the publication of this book. Most importantly, I would like to thank Namarita Kathait of SAGE for reading the initial drafts and advising on improving the quality of write-ups.

—**Manu Sharma**

Introduction

The book covers the fundamental aspects of venture capital (VC). These fundamental aspects include the definition of VC, history of VC, VC industry in India, deal evaluation by venture capitalists, valuation of VC investments, fund structure of VC firms, fund economics of VC rewards and fundraising by venture capitalists.

In Chapter 1, we will discuss the concept of VC. Also, we will discuss the technical differences between venture debt and venture equity. Lastly, the characteristics of VC investments, including illiquidity, information asymmetry and cyclicality, will be discussed.

In Chapter 2, we will discuss the history of VC in global as well as Indian perspective.

In Chapter 3, we will discuss the VC industry, key players in VC and few successful deals in the VC industry in India. The VC industry will be discussed in terms of its importance in global as well as Indian perspective. The key players in the VC industry, which invests in start-ups in India, will be discussed along with few key deals in the Indian VC industry.

In Chapter 4, we will discuss the deal evaluation process followed by the venture capitalists while evaluating a potential investment opportunity. There are five parts of the deal evaluation process, and these parts include opportunities in the market, competitive edge, the team of a start-up, uniqueness of investment opportunity in a start-up and deal characteristics.

In Chapter 5, we will discuss the start-up valuation using two approaches including market-approach-based valuation and discounted cash flow-based valuation. The market-approach-based valuations focus on using multiple, which is either generated by dividing enterprise value by any of the variants including revenue, earnings before interest and taxes (EBIT) or earnings before interest, tax, depreciation and amortization (EBITDA) or generated by dividing the market value of equity by net income, that is, using price to earnings ratio. The discounted cash-flow valuation focuses on determining the value of business by calculating the present value of free cash flow to the firm (FCFF).

In Chapter 6, we will discuss the structure of VC funds and will learn about the functioning of various involved parties, including a management company, limited partner and general partner. The chapter will also discuss different types of VC funds and investments by such funds in portfolio companies. Lastly, the chapter will also cover the structure of investment holdings and steps involved in funding portfolio companies.

In Chapter 7, we will discuss the fund economics of VC firms and how different participants play their respective roles in fund economics. The discussion will revolve around primary funders of fund economics and how hurdle rate, carried interest, escrow and clawback agreements play a crucial role in fund economics. Lastly, as part of fund economics, we will discuss the exit route of investments.

In Chapter 8, we will discuss how VC firms (general partners) raise capital for their respective funds. The fundraising process revolves around the prospectus of the fund, and so an in-depth discussion regarding preparation of prospectus will be explained. The prospectus has two crucial factors including the team of VC fund and fund intricacies and details and so these two factors are discussed in detail.

1

WHAT IS
VENTURE CAPITAL?

everal factors have contributed to an increase in businesses and business-minded people all over the world. One of the most significant factors contributing to this increase is globalization and the ability to sell things quickly through the Internet to any corner of the world. While this increase in business opportunities might seem like an ideal way to improve the economy, job market and overall condition of the standard of living, at the same time, these businesses need to have access to various factors of production, most crucial being the capital. There are several sources through which an individual or a new starter can source a business.[1] Before accessing any of those sources, it is necessary to understand the pros and cons of each one of them so that the individual has a better understanding of which one to utilize.

One of the most common and important sources that can be utilized is venture capital (VC). This is ideal for individuals who are looking for financial support to start a new business. It is a sort of growth or start-up capital or loan that is provided by institutions that are specialized in this sort of funding or by individuals who provide private funds. VC is also known as risk capital.[2] These individuals and institutes are focused on developing a portfolio that is focused on high-risk and high-return concept.

1 Gibbons, Hisrich, and DaSilva, *Entrepreneurial Finance*.
2 Mishra and Chary, *Venture Capital Financing for Biotechnology*.

Researching and understanding various aspects of VC would help the readers and prospective entrepreneurs to develop an understanding of how to apply for VC as well as to attract venture capitalists, who are the investors, to invest their funds in several start-ups.

VC is an essential source of financing for start-up/immature companies. Although it requires time and patience, it is beneficial for companies in several ways. The venture capitalists do not only provide the start-ups with financial support but they also provide them with necessary mentorship and help with managing the business effectively and efficiently. It is the responsibility of the general partners (GPs) to ensure that the limited partners (LPs) benefit from the investments and that the management of the start-up does not make any decision which would have a negative impact on the investment. Thus, start-ups benefit from both the capital and the expertise of running the start-up provided by venture capitalists. This makes entrepreneurs run the start-ups efficiently and comfortably.

As it is a form of equity financing, the entrepreneurs would not have to face the same burden that they would have faced in the case of borrowing a loan from a financial institution. This would help them focus on the growth and expansion of the business, which would generate better returns, as they would not have to worry about paying back the money along with interest after a specific time. The investors in case of VC would only be paid back in case of an initial public offering (IPO), a merger or an acquisition. Thus, the entrepreneurs would not have to take out the cash that could have been used for other aspects of the business.

VENTURE DEBT VERSUS VENTURE EQUITY

The companies raise cash in the form of capital so as to generate assets. These assets are used to run a given company by bumping in the capital. The capital can be raised either in the form of equity or debt. The equity capital defines the share of equity holders in a given company and so if the majority of the capital is raised through equity then the company is said to be less leveraged, and if the majority of the capital is raised through debt, then the company is said to be highly leveraged. To check whether the majority of capital is raised through equity, we divide the total equity of the company by total assets of the company. If the ratio is less than 50 per cent then majority of assets are created by raising debt, and if the ratio is greater than 50 per cent then majority of assets are created by raising equity. In case of liquidation of a given company, debt holders are the first ones to receive a claim on assets and so equity holders receive a residual claim on assets. The equity to assets ratio is stated as equity holders' ratio and can also be interpreted that wealth equity holders will receive in case of liquidation of the respective company.

The debt obligations mean whether the company has strength in its assets to convert these assets into cash and pay off debt. The short-term debt obligations are those loans that expire in less than a year. Such loans are taken for working capital expenditure. The long-term debt obligations are the loans which are availed for a more extended time and do not expire in less than a year. Generally, such loans are availed for capital expenditure including property, plant and equipment. The debt capital ratio helps in determining the percentage of debt and equity used by the respective company so as to finance its assets. The debt capital ratio also helps in determining the percentage of debt in the total capital structure of the company. It is determined by dividing long-term debt with the sum of long-term debt and total equity of the company. The long-term debt and total equity are the forms of capital that provide long-term total capital for a given company. The debt holders provide loans at a specific interest rate and so upside gain of these lenders is limited to the interest rate charged on loan. The companies raise a specific part of their capital in the form of debt, so that the majority of their wealth is transferred to a smaller number of shareholders. This activity helps in achieving stakeholder value maximization. Also, companies raise debt with the intention of financing a specific stable future cash flows with debt. By this, we mean that if the companies know that a specific part of their total cash flows is stable in the future, then the companies would like to finance such part with debt as the upside gain for such lenders is limited to interest expense and a more significant portion of the gain will be transferred to shareholders.

Moreover, in the income statement, the interest expense is paid before the taxes are paid and so, a certain level of debt in the capital structure provides tax benefits to the respective companies. Many companies work on determining their optimal capital structure which is a structure at which the tax benefits are maximum. So, there are many reasons to have debt in the capital structure of the company.

However, the optimal capital structure is not the only structure every company chooses to operate with. Many remain below or above depending upon the nature of the business, type of industry and market conditions. The more is the percentage of stability in future cash flows, the more is the debt. Also, for different industries and companies in different phases of capital market life cycles, there are a different amount of debt capital requirements. The one single debt ratio is not an appropriate way of measuring the financial health of the companies and all the industries across the globe. The investors should study all the above parameters before using debt ratio as a tool to understand the financial health of a company. Although different companies in different industries and different phases are analysed differently in terms of amount of capital financed through debt and riskiness it brings in terms of solvency, the higher levels of debt is not recommended in any given start-up company as long-term debt demands interest payments at regular intervals over the life of the loan.

As discussed earlier, a company raises capital in the form of equity and/or debt so as to run its operations. The debt is raised in the form of loans from financial institutions, and equity is raised from investors.

The debt to equity ratio helps in calculating levered beta (β) of a given company which in turn helps in determining the cost of equity of a given company. The cost of equity is the percentage of return a company is supposed to provide to its investors depending upon the riskiness of an investment in its equity. The investors can compare the cost of equity of a company with a return on equity of that company so as to analyse whether the company has outperformed, fairly performed or underperformed. A company outperforms when the return on equity is higher than the cost of equity. A company fairly performs when the return on equity equals the cost of equity, and it underperforms when the return on equity is less than the cost of equity. The cost of equity is used as a discounting factor to find the present value of future free cash flows to the equity holders. The present value of future free cash flows to equity holders, in turn, helps in determining the share price of the start-up company's equity. Also, the cost of equity helps in understanding as to how risky is an investment with respect to the return on investment.

The long-term debt is used to finance noncurrent assets, and by long-term debt we mean the debt takes more than one year to expire. For example, if a company has raised total long-term debt of ₹2 billion and has total assets of ₹5 billion then long-term debt to total assets ratio would be 0.4 (₹2 billion/₹5 billion). This means that for every ₹100 invested in the operations of the company, ₹40 is financed by long-term debt.

Higher long-term debt to equity ratio means that it will be harder for the company to raise debt in the future and so current projects should be sufficient enough to raise enough cash flows to pay off debt as well as generate returns for shareholders. Lower long-term debt to equity ratio does not necessarily mean that the company is a good investment as investors have to evaluate current and future projects of the company so as to understand the future cash flows that will be generated by the company.

Also, even in good economic conditions, the larger amount of debt is considered risky as the competition with other companies might fluctuate the operating income which can lead to an inability of the company to pay off its interest expense commitments. However, many start-up companies carry a certain amount of debt in their capital structure and still are considered less risky because of the strategic standing of the company in the market. Strategic standing means that the company has strong, stable and predictable cash flows, brand image, consumer loyalty and is reluctant to raise capital in the form of equity. Whenever the capital requirements in a given company are met by issuing new equity capital, then dilution of the share of promoters happen. To avoid such dilution, the promoters choose debt over equity.

The VC investments are highly risky in nature because such investments are done in ideas and/or immature start-ups. The immature start-up companies are in nascent start with no revenue at all. Such immature companies need capital so as to build technologies/prototype. The venture capitalists choose to pick up such ideas/immature companies where if the technology is developed, then it will be a game changer in capital markets. The VC investments are done in the form of equity, and these equity investments are made where there is a certain level of probability that if the venture becomes successful, then the respective idea/immature company will be worth billion dollars. As the capital investment by venture capitalists is in the form of equity, there is no specific incentives that will be received at a particular time of intervals, unlike debt. If the venture becomes successful, then the valuation of start-up improves exponentially, and so venture capitalist could sell his/her stake and realize a profit.

CHARACTERISTICS OF VC INVESTMENTS

The characteristics of VC investments can be classified into three factors, including illiquidity, information asymmetry and cyclicality

Figure 1.1 Characteristics of Venture Capital

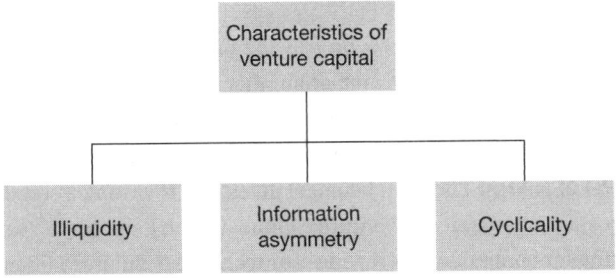

(Figure 1.1). The illiquidity governs as to how hard it is for an investor to exit an investment made in the past. The information asymmetry governs the disparity various players have in the financial markets. There are many industries which are cyclical in nature whereby the companies in the industry see upward and downward trends of performance on a cyclical basis.

Illiquidity in VC Investments

Some shares trade more actively than others on stock exchanges implying there is more of a market for them. Those shares attract greater and more consistent interest from traders and investors, meaning they have more liquidity which is usually identifiable by their daily volume. Liquidity is defined as the ability to purchase or sell an asset quickly at a price close to its fair market value. Liquidity can be measured by trading volume or bid-ask spreads. In the event of a stock market crash or financial distress, the stocks might become relatively illiquid reflected through lower trading volume and the wider bid-ask spreads. Liquidity afforded by markets for publicly-traded shares allows investors to diversify their portfolios at a lower cost. Investors must consider an essential trade-off between yield and liquidity. Illiquidity helps earn illiquidity premium and hence higher yields. However, market data including price and volume data necessary to evaluate liquidity are not readily available for VC deals.

The equity financing of new or growing private companies is VC. A closely held business with smaller number of owners, could be family members or unrelated, may come together to seek help from outside investors for professional managerial skills, diversity, monetary help or IPO of shares. They can be angel investors, investing in seed and early stage companies or venture capitalists who have pooled capital looking for companies having ideas or technology but need financial, managerial and strategic support or any large company. Venture capitalists mostly buy stakes in an entrepreneur's idea; nurture it in the best possible manner with its resources and then exit. Paytm might not have possibly come through if someone at SAIF Partners would not have believed in Vijay Shekhar Sharma's business acumen. Similarly, Oyo—the idea of a college dropout, Ritesh Agarwal—would not have been a success without someone's faith in Lightspeed Venture Partners. According to PricewaterhouseCoopers International Limited (PwC), an investment of approximately $59.7 billion was made in USA in VC and €11.1 billion in Pan-Europe in 2015. A global private equity fund, General Atlantic, has been a major player providing capital and strategic support for the growth of companies by investing $2.6 billion in 27 Indian companies and has realized $2.4 billion from the exit of 13 investments.

In VC, patience and reposing faith are crucial to success. It is fascinating to be the angel investor or venture capitalists, but do they actually make steady returns and how long is it before they get liquidity? A liquidity event is a merger or an acquisition, IPO or another event that allows founders and investors to cash out some or all of their ownership shares. It is considered as an exit strategy for an illiquid investment. According to CB Insights, the average time for venture capitalists to exit via IPO is seven years and via Mergers and acquisitions (M&A) is five years. According to the National Stock

Exchange (NSE), FY 2017–2018 has been a historic year for Indian primary market which witnessed Indian corporates garnering funds to the tune of ₹905.64 billion, majority of them being exits by private equity/venture capitalist. VC is a long-term commitment of funds, structured in the form of direct or indirect investments with an investor being fully prepared to lock funds for an extended period. Direct investments are typically structured in the form of convertible preferred stocks that usually do not trade in a secondary market. For those that do, they trade at highly discounted prices making the exit position an unattractive option. This stock often comes with a liquidation preference providing downside protection to investors, ensuring that in a liquidity event, they get a certain return on their money before any equity claimant. It mitigates the risk that the company will take on VC investment and distribute it to the owner or promoter. The liquidation preference is typically expressed as a multiple of the original invested capital, usually at 1x. So, in the event of a sale of the company, the investor will be entitled to receive back $1 for every $1 invested, in preference to the holders of common stock. For risky companies, the investors may ask for a higher liquidation preference, say 1.5× or 2×. Indirect investment through VC funds is usually structured as limited partnerships with an expected life span of 7–10 years. Venture capitalists get liquidity after the general partner is expected to realize the value of the investments by the fund's liquidation date. An early exit from a VC fund inevitably leads to paramount losses. It is precisely the illiquidity that enables investors to earn illiquidity premium, and hence significant returns. In addition to this, VC can bring diversification to one's investment portfolio driven by low correlation with traditional asset classes including stocks and bonds.

Let us consider an example: ABC co. plans to acquire XYZ co. for ₹1,100 million. XYZ stakes include 70 per cent to entrepreneur (promoters) and 30 per cent to VC firm. VC firm funded ₹150 million amount thus valuing the company at ₹500 million. In this, venture capitalists holding preference shares will be paid out first, implying out of ₹1,100 million, ₹150 million is paid to fund. Further, if the company has declared any dividend, say ₹35 million, then it has to be paid and the remaining ₹915 million will get distributed in the ratio 7:3, that is, entrepreneurs get ₹640.5 million and venture capitalists get ₹274.5 million. The calculation of amount made: it initially invested ₹150 million but gets ₹424.5 million amount for 30 per cent stake, making a 2.8 multiple. So, they almost got 39 per cent returns despite having 30 per cent stake.

US-based multinational hospitality company Airbnb has recently announced its plans to become a publicly listed company in 2020. At a conference in May 2018, Airbnb's chief executive officer Brian Chesky said, 'We have investors who are patient, and I want to make sure it is a benefit when we do.' The agenda is to keep the faith of the investors that have helped Airbnb become a behemoth. Venture capitalists follow the Pareto principle—80 per cent of the wins come from 20 per cent of the deals. Most of the VC firms rely on a few lucrative exits. Ride-hailing giant, Uber, saw a plunge in stock immediately at the opening of trading and many venture capitalists who had piled into the company were saddled with losses.

Venture capitalist investment in a start-up is more or less about operational improvements, new hires, funding runway, product/ market fit and customer acquisition strategies. However, for most, the prospect of an eventual exit is also always present, no matter how far futuristic it might be. Liquidity in VC is a very long tail and is all about its timing. Some of the biggest winners may take 10–15 years to IPO to exit. Illiquidity of VC affects the value of an investor's interest. The value determined by models such as VC method or discounted cash flow may be used as an estimate of the value for a marketable controlling interest. However, if the owner has a minority interest and the equity interest does not have a ready market, then discounts are often applied to reflect the diminished value. The discount for lack of marketability takes account of the lack of liquidity in the investment and depends on several factors, such as the size of the interest and the level of dividends paid. Calculation of a non-marketable minority interest: the equity of co. MN has a value of $600 million if it were publicly traded. Mr B intends to make 10 per cent investment in co. MN. The minority interest discount of 25 per cent and a marketability discount of 20 per cent are deemed appropriate. The value of the investment by Mr B will be (600×0.1) $(1 - 0.25)(1 - 0.2) = \$36$ million.

The investors typically prefer delayed exits of sufficient size over less successful pre-planned liquidity events. Such exits provide steady payoffs to venture capitalists as exemplified by Microsoft's acquisition of GitHub for $7.5 billion in 2018. With this in mind, an opposite trend was seen in the USA where the exit markets strengthened in 2018 primarily to provide liquidity than raising funds. This could be supported by Spotify that went public on 3 April 2018 through a direct listing of its shares on New York Stock Exchange (NYSE) instead of a traditional IPO with an aim to provide unrestricted access to all buyers and sellers, hence allowing its existing shareholders the ability to sell their shares immediately after listing at market price. Spotify was able to provide liquidity while not imposing IPO-style lock-up agreements upon listing. Liquidity options continue to increase for VC in the form of IPO that many tech firms including Spotify, Dropbox have opted or buyouts by private equity firms and M&A. Another trend has come up where some investors may exit while the company remains private. It relieves the pressure to rush to the exit door and allows large investors to sell to another investor or late-stage VC fund that wants pre-IPO exposure. Some of the companies are taking private investment rounds and then doing secondary on the back of that. A secondary sale would allow a shareholder of a private company to sell the shares to another buyer. It usually happens when the start-up has achieved significant success but is still on its way to an IPO. It is different from a primary sale or IPO where the company issues new shares.

The main drivers behind secondaries include the following scenario: when the investors want to get hold of the equity in the company, but the start-up may not require funding, that is, mismatch between demand and supply to liquidity for shareholders. The most popular buyers of the private secondary are usually either existing investors or new investors in a round of financing. Early seed-stage funds, especially ones that have only raised one or two funds, almost view that as their IPO opportunity. For example, Zynga Inc., an American social game developer did an approximately $500 million financing round before IPO which included a certain amount set aside for early employees and founders. Venture capitalists take on liquidity risk with a view of achieving significant returns. The first two quarters of 2018 have seen late stage funding to be over 20 per cent of total VC, well above from previous years because companies are staying private longer and venture capitalists want to secure funds when sacrificing liquidity.

VC fund prefers not to exit in an untimely fashion due to expected J-curve pattern of interim returns over the life of VC fund. Investors realize cash flows later due to longer than usual cash burning stage. The returns are usually negative for initial years as the portfolio of companies continue to grow and progress resulting in cash burn, but later the returns accelerate as the companies are exited. Valuation of companies considers a discount for lack of liquidity, which depends on factors such as the shareholding structure, the level of profitability, expected sustainability, the possibility of IPO in the near future and the size of private company. The demand for VC funds can be either by formative stage companies such as Practo, Grofers and PepperTap that received funding through Sequoia Capital or by expansion stage companies such as MakeMyTrip (MMT), TaxiFor-Sure that received funds from Helion Venture Partners.

Good things come with time, and this is the due reward to VC investors. Let us consider the example of WhatsApp, a big win for

Sequoia Capital which was the only venture investor of the company. Sequoia believed in WhatsApp future success and was the sole investor in both $8 million series A round in 2011 and subsequent $52 million Series B round in 2013. Sequoia's well-known trajectory helped it beat the micro-VC fund and by the time Facebook acquired WhatsApp for $22 billion, Sequoia's 18 per cent ownership was worth more than $3 billion, a 50x return overall with an investment of $60 million. VC firms get rewarded for making accurate predictions and identifying a pattern before it becomes a trend. Although there is liquidity risk, there is always a scope for earning steady returns for patient venture capitalists.

Cyclicality in Venture Capital

The financial markets do not move up linearly and continue to grow by creating new troughs (upward movement) and new crests (downward movement) as it moves upwards. As time continues to move, the markets continue to grow but by creating new troughs and crests. These troughs and crests signify the condition of the market in terms of good economic conditions and adverse economic conditions. When the financial market is going through a good phase in a booming state, then market forms new troughs and when the financial market is going through a rough phase in a slowdown state, then market forms new crests. These troughs and crests reflect the cyclicality of movements in financial markets as there is good cycle and adverse cycle. The cyclicality governs the entry, exit and profitability of VC investments (Figure 1.2). Let us now discuss as to how cyclicality influences entry, exit and profitability of VC investments.

If a venture capitalist plans to enter into an investment at a time when financial markets are booming, then the biggest challenge is to get into an investment at the right valuation. This is because of the fact that during the booming time in an economy the valuations

Figure 1.2 Cyclicality in Venture Capital

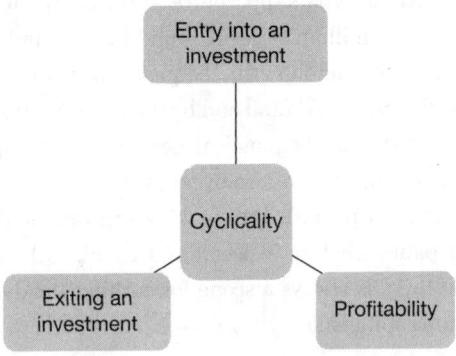

are performed using aggressive assumptions. These aggressive assumptions tend to over value the investments because of overvaluation of start-up/immature companies. This makes a point of entry giving a lesser amount of stake for a more significant amount of capital. However, VC investments are long term in nature, and an investment in a company has to hold for more than one cycle to create significant value irrespective of the fact as to when the venture capitalist has entered into an investment in a start-up, the start-up has to survive, prosper and create value in a complete cycle in order to be a successful investment. Therefore, an investment done in a booming market environment might end up exiting in a slowdown environment which means at the time of slowdown, the valuation assumptions are passive in nature and so investment might not be carrying as much value as the same investment would have carried in booming economic conditions. In particular, there can be a difference of multiple of five or more in exit valuations of an investee company depending on the stage of the market cycle.

The valuations are not the only thing that influences the profitability at the time of exit. At the exit, the venture capitalist either sells the stake to another investor or whole company is sold as an acquisition deal. In the market slowdown, it might be easier to find investors who are willing to buy stake because such investors know that they are buying stakes at relatively cheaper valuations as the actual value of an investment is not reflected in slowdown. However, in a slowdown, there is relatively a lesser number of investors available to buy the business for the purpose of acquisition as bigger companies make such acquisitions. Such companies reduce their mergers and acquisition activity during market slowdown. However, good companies are efficient in nature in terms of creating value for its stakeholders and so even in adverse market conditions, such companies can still create good exit value for its investors. From the venture capitalist point of view in good market conditions, it is easier to raise capital and hard to find good start-up/immature companies with great ideas. This is because of the fact that these good start-up/immature companies are getting investment offers from the most influential and capable venture capitalists.

If a venture capitalist plans to enter into an investment at a time when market is in slowdown, then getting into an investment at right valuation is no more a challenge. This is because of the fact that during slowdown time in the economy the valuations are performed using passive assumptions. These passive assumptions tend to undervalue the investments because of the undervaluation of start-up/immature companies. This makes a point of entry giving a higher amount of stake for a lesser amount of capital. However, VC investments are long term in nature, and an investment in a company has to hold for more than one cycle to create significant value. Irrespective of the fact as to when the venture capitalist has entered into an investment in a start-up, the start-up has to survive, prosper and create value in the complete cycle in order to be a successful investment. Therefore, an investment done in the market slowdown environment might end up exiting in a booming market environment. At the time of booming market, valuation assumptions are aggressive in nature, and so investment will carry far more value than same investment would have carried in slowdown market conditions.

In particular, there can be a difference of multiple of 10 or more in exit valuations of an investee company depending on the stage of the market cycle. The valuations are not the only thing that influences the profitability at the time of exit. At the exit, the venture capitalist either sells the stake to another investor or whole company is sold as an acquisitions deal. In a booming market state, it is easier to sell the business as an acquisition by another company. The premium paid to buy the business is high, and so the venture capitalist can expect exponential returns from an investment. The above-mentioned timing of entering at slowdown and exiting during the booming market will generate exponential returns by investing in good companies only. Only good companies are efficient in nature in terms of creating value for its stakeholders and so in the booming market, such companies can create extraordinary exit value for its investors. From the venture capitalist point of view in market slowdown conditions, it is very difficult to raise capital and find good start-up/immature companies with great ideas. This is because liquidity decreases during the slowdown, and few investors have enough cash to invest in start-up/immature companies. Therefore, apart from identifying good start-up/immature companies to generate returns for their investors, the venture capitalists also have to work on timing the market so as to generate maximum returns for themselves.

2 HISTORY OF VENTURE CAPITAL

V C is a type of private equity-based financing in which funding is provided to the firms of varying sizes which are seen to have high growth potential in the future. These firms are considered to have high value and growth for all its stakeholders. They are expected to see an exponential rise in their profitability and revenue in the near future. There are specialized venture capitalist firms which look to invest in these firms at an early stage in exchange for equity or a share in these firms. As the firm grows, the venture capitalist company is expected to see rising profits in return for its investment being carried out. The return being earned by the venture capitalist companies is in return for the risk they undertake for financing such a company. The start-up funded can be seen as a good prospect, but with a start-up there is a great risk attached to it as it can fail, and its future is seen to be highly uncertain.[1]

Based on their nature, many start-ups and venture capitalist investments see a high rate of failure as they are based on an innovative new technology or a business model which has not been seen before. Their success is dependent on the industry, either adapting the new technology or the business model. Many start-ups nowadays tend to fail than succeed because they are solely centred

1 Malmström, Johansson, and Wincent, 'Gender Stereotypes and Venture Support Decisions', 833–860.

on technology. Venture capitals usually enter the investment cycle at the seed funding stage where the venture capitalist carries out the first investment into the company. The venture capitalist knows that the investment being made will be for a certain amount of time and can only expect any payout for the investment once the start-up reaches its exit stage or event.[2] These events take place in the form of an IPO or a merger and acquisition of the company to another.

The exit stage can also come in the form of the secondary market through a private equity firm as well. Venture capitalists can facilitate a portion of the market which is seen to be too small or too risky for traditional debt and equity financing, and they cater to a market which needs equity-based financing for some time.[3] The venture capitalists can fund such a market but require a high return in exchange as they are taking on a large amount of risk. The risk is the highest at the seeding stage where the idea or start-up is just starting, and their success cannot be determined. As the start-up progresses and the success of the start-up is determined, it is seen that the risk decreases while the return earned also decreases.[4] This type of venture capitalism is known as a unicorn. In order to attract venture capitalists, the start-ups have to give up a significant part of their control over the company in return of the financing where the venture capitalists provide financing and advice the firm's executive in their business model and marketing strategies.

HISTORY OF GLOBAL VENTURE CAPITALISM

Even though the start-up industry today cannot be fathomed without a VC industry, the roots of the modern-day venture capitalism dates back to many decades ago. In the past, entrepreneurs had to

2 Bernstein, Giroud, and Townsend, 'The Impact of Venture Capital Monitoring', 1591–1622.
3 Bottazzi, Da Rin, and Hellmann, 'The Importance of Trust for Investment', 2283–2318.
4 Mollick and Robb, 'Democratizing Innovation and Capital Access', 72–87.

look towards debt financing for their companies. The debt lenders volunteered to finance on the basis of strict conditions as they needed the safety and security of being paid back in time by the entrepreneurs. Equity-based investment was seen as being inherently risky in terms of return on investment on the capital invested into the start-up. Hurdles to equity investment were the fact that the information systems were outdated and inaccurate so the profit of a company could not be calculated while shareholders had unlimited liability meaning they could end up losing an amount higher than their investment in case the company went bankrupt.[5] Even after the development of information systems and limited liability laws, equity investment was hard to attract as start-ups needed a way to advertise their ventures and make them look attractive.

By the start of the 20th century, investors were only looking to invest in companies with sizeable tangible asset base or retail businesses due to their recurring revenue stream which made them look valuable.[6] Ventures which focused on technological advancement did not feature as an attractive company to invest in while banks were not looking to businesses whose future was uncertain and the business model was unknown. Public equity-based financing was also not an option as such businesses could not be valued based on no or little revenue stream in the early stages of development. This gap had to be filled and was carried out by venture capitalists who were wealthy individuals running merchant banks and were willing to invest their riches. Some of the early venture capitalists included Lazard's André Meyer and Lionel Pincus who could carry out such investments. Due to lack of such investments, the government had to step in and fill the role of financing such activities.

5 Gompers, Gornall, Kaplan, and Strebulaev, 'How Do Venture Capitalists Make Decisions?', 169–190.
6 Chemmanur, Hull, and Krishnan, 'Do Local and International Venture Capitalists Play Well Together?', 573–594.

After the start of the Second World War, it was seen that America lagged behind the forces of Japan and Germany as many of the researchers wanted to be a part of the academia rather than the military. The problem was solved by funding the research departments of some of the elite universities of the country which led to newcutting-edge technologies being developed. Once the war ended, the funding carried on and led to the development of entrepreneurs resulting into a post war boom in the country.[7] Seeing this boom, investors started to invest in new ventures which led to a large-scale investment being carried out in companies which were technological in nature. The whole country saw investment being carried out in terms of research and development of ideas which were needed in the market but were too uncertain in regard to their future prospects.

The formal recognition of VC as an asset class was seen in the 1970s with the start of the personal computing industry. By now, it was seen that through proper funding in the seeding stage and backing by the investors, companies could be grown from a start-up and they could be taken public which meant that there was a defined entry and exit phase for a venture capitalist. Furthermore, to align the goals between the management and the investor to lead to a common goal, the managers were given incentives which were outlined in a legal form. As the personal computing market was starting to grow with the launch of computers such as Apple II, VC started to see exponential growth in investments which saw complimentary financial market-based solutions such as leveraged buyouts. As the industry grew, these leverage buyouts started to gain momentum. This trend being carried forward to the 1990s was courtesy tech bubble which flourished throughout the decade.

7 Chernenko, Lerner, and Zeng, *Mutual Funds as Venture Capitalists?*

Venture Capitalism in India

In terms of its history in India, it has been seen that venture capitalism plays an essential role in the development and growth of entrepreneurship in the country. The start of venture capitalism in India can be traced back to the early 1970s when the government of India appointed a committee under Shri R. S. Bhatt to find ways to fill in the gap that existed between traditional financing and funding for start-up companies. The focus of the committee was to look at companies which were involved in the manufacturing of innovative technologies. The committee recommended the establishment of a VC industry in India which led to the introduction of VC financing in 1975 with the formation of the Industrial Finance Corporation of India. By 1976, Industrial Development Bank of India had also started a seed capital scheme which continued till 1984 and was responsible for taking on risk and providing seed capital.

In 1985, a fund was set up by the government of India, which was responsible for providing equity capital for firms and projects which were commercial in nature but were connected to innovative technologies.[8] It was not until 1986 that venture capitalism got formal recognition in the fiscal budget of the country where a cess of 5 per cent was levied on the know-how imports of the country in order to create a fund for VC related activities. By 1987, Industrial Development Bank of India introduced a scheme to finance VCs which were looking to import foreign technology and providing a more extensive commercial application of those technologies. The goal of this scheme was not only to benefit the venture capitalists but also to provide an implementation plan of foreign technologies to take place on a domestic level. This would prove to create new opportunities to the local market

8 Hellmann, Schure, and Vo, 'Angels and Venture Capitalists: Complements or Substitutes?'.

and would provide a far more significant benefit to the country.[9] By the end of 1985, three of the leading Indian financial institutions, Industrial Development Bank of India, Industrial Finance Corporation of India and ICICI, were investing equity into start-up companies all over India.

As the growth of financing of start-ups was taking place, the government of India wanted to formulate guidelines which supervised the VC funds. In order to do so, the Controller of Capital Issues issued guidelines regarding VC funds which defined what VC funds were and made sure that only national level financial institutions and scheduled commercial banks were involved in setting up such funds. An advisory committee set under Dr Ashok Lahiri concluded that international start-ups were set up by professional entrepreneurs and were funded by venture capitalists who could take the higher risks associated with the start-ups.[10] The guidelines made the investments in the start-ups run by first generation entrepreneurs highly risky and unattractive for venture capitalists. However, once the liberalization of the economy took place, the foreign venture capitalists were attracted to the Indian market, and the Securities and Exchange Commission of India was now responsible for governing and supervising the VC industry of India.

In the early stages of formalization, India had set out to institutionalize the VC industry structure. After the liberalization of the economy, foreign investors started to enter the market and led to significant investment being carried out in the industry starting from 1995. The growth in the Indian VC industry can be seen from 1995 till now where information technology boom and investment from foreign VC

9 Colombo, Cumming, and Vismara, 'Governmental Venture Capital for Innovative Young Firms', 10–24.
10 Klausner and Litvak, 'What Economists Have Taught Us about Venture Capital Contracting', 54–74.

companies have led to where the industry stands today. The trend of investment in the VC industry is seen as falling from 1998 to 2001 as the IT boom subsided, but then the bulk of capital was invested after 2001. The bursting of the dotcom bubble and the 9/11 taking place in 2001 led to a fall in fund raising activities taking place in the USA and a simultaneous fall in investment in India. The country felt the impact because around 90 per cent of the investment taking place here was from the USA. From 2001 to 2003, the investors looked to invest in more mature companies which had proven their success in order to minimize their risk exposure to the industry.

During this time, the industry was looking to recover and saw a slow rise in investment being carried out at the seed stage of the start-ups.[11] As the fund raising started to recover in the USA from 2003 onwards, the impact of this was seen in the leading and emerging markets of China and India where the investment had started to take place. As the Indian market prospered, its growth led to the re-emergence of interest and confidence in the market and the consequent reinvestment by the investors. VC investment saw substantial growth from 2005 onwards as the USA and Indian economy moved in tandem towards growth. This growth hit another stumbling block in 2008 when the USA saw the sub-prime mortgage crisis take place.[12] This led to a quick fall of US VC investment and the VC industry saw the liquidity market dry up.

The liquidity present in the world economy saw a sharp decline and the investors were not willing to invest in new ventures because of the limited financial resources. As the financial situations of the start-ups were impacted, they saw decline in their earnings and valuations, and their economic outlook was uncertain for the short term. Start-ups were seen to be uncertain in terms of investment

11 Hisrich, Petković, Ramadani, and Dana, 'Venture Capital Funds in Transition Countries', 296–315.
12 Manigart and Sapienza, 'Venture Capital and Growth', 240–258.

horizon and return, and investors were more willing to invest directly in the listed companies as this left their investment to be liquid for easy withdrawal.

The decade since 2010 has seen another explosion of start-ups, entrepreneurship and has given a new lease of life to many of the venture capitalists looking to invest in the Indian market. The new start-up landscape has gone global rather than staying local with the use of smartphones increasing from 2005 to 2019, and there is a higher probability that start-ups are now competing with each other on a global scale.[13] The Indian start-up industry has spawned its own start-up companies such as Ola, Zomato, Swiggy which are now able to compete with Uber and Airbnb on their own.[14] The fact that these companies are set up in India and have an understanding of the local market means that they can cater to the needs and demands of their customers in a much better manner. In some cases, these local start-ups are preferred to the international counterparts as they are better in the local market as compared to their global substitutes.

The success of learning app Byju is another excellent example of innovation being carried out. The idea of the application was to design a learning app for school going children which could help them learn key concepts and ideas that they were already learning in school. The additional education tools added a visual aspect to the idea of learning and helped children in a new manner. The services provided by the application have now grown to even include small classes as the application gained more prominence and hits.[15] The success of the company shows that there is a future in the Indian start-up market. Gradually, as this industry will thrive the VC industry,

13 Cumming, Henriques, and Sadorsky, '"Cleantech" Venture Capital Around the World', 86–97.
14 Wallmeroth, Wirtz, and Groh, 'Venture Capital, Angel Financing, and Crowdfunding of Entrepreneurial Ventures', 1–129.
15 Zi-yao, 'Do Corporate Venture Capitalists Add Value to Start-up Firms', 4.

it will be needed in order to fund such ideas and start-ups in the long run.

Venture capitalists around the world have a significant role to play in terms of their involvement in the financial landscape of the global economy. They have the responsibility to take one additional risk and invest in the horizon which is not favoured by traditional means of financing. This means that in order to fund the engine of innovation, there will always be some form of financing that they will have to carry out. History of venture capitalists has shown that even though start-ups are seen to be risky and uncertain, the growth and potential that they have makes them viable enough to be funded by venture capitalists. For every start-up that has failed, there is a Facebook or Google which has succeeded and has changed the way people think of start-ups. The same case can be applied to the Indian VC industry. From 1975 to till now, the industry has come a long way. Even though the future of a VC industry can be seen to be unpredictable and uncertain, it can be seen that the industry in India is growing and has enormous potential. With the development of companies such as Ola, Zomato, Flipkart, the country has shown that there is an enormous market for start-ups and as long as there are start-ups, the VC industry will be required to fund the industry.

3 VENTURE CAPITAL INDUSTRY

The VC industry is a key ingredient for global as well as country-wise economic growth. The general objectives of the venture capitalists are to generate capital gains that come as a result of high returns from the development of a portfolio.[1] Typically, this involves providing equity at an early age of the business to accelerate economic growth and development. To achieve this goal, the firms involved in VC ensure that there is a constant flow of capital, advice and other critical conditions that are needed in a country. Companies that meet the minimum conditions to receive VC plays an important role in the development of the region where they are located by supporting the growth of jobs as well as the expansion of the tax base.

VC promotes the creation of new technology and industries that did not exist in the economy. In the 1970s, the biotechnology industry started as a result of investment in Genentech and Amgen. Ten years later, the concept of VC has spread in semiconductor software development industries. One of the most recent growths as a result of the VC is the concept of online retailing.[2] To add on that, the VC firms tend to cluster in one region where they come up with new technologies and ease the process of doing business in the location.[3]

---

1 ABC Investments, 'Role of Venture Capital in the Economic Growth of the United States'.
2 IHS Global Insight, *Venture Impact*.
3 Mason and Harrison, 'Improving Access to Early Stage Venture Capital in Regional Economies'.

For example, the VC industry in Ottawa was developed as a result of technology that was available in the location. New technology means that the production of goods and services will increase in the region where the firms are located. The increase in production creates employment for the locals, hence improving their living standards. Furthermore, the growth of new firms compels the government to improve the general infrastructure of the area, and hence facilitate economic development.

The huge economic development in the USA is highly associated with VC investments from individuals as well as companies. The venture capitalists have largely facilitated communication technologies, innovations as well as access to new critical information in the market. Furthermore, VC is also described as the backbone of the successive capitalistic economy of the USA. A research conducted by Stanford University found out that 38 per cent of the employed people in the country are from venture-backed companies.[4] This huge employment created by the concept of VC cannot be neglected as one of the key factors to economic growth in the country. Romer[5] proposed that economic growth in any nation is determined by the changes in technology that come as a result of the intentional investment made by either the government or any local investor. Therefore, the economic growth of the USA and other countries with a big number of ventures-backed companies can be explained using this concept.

Second, VC has played a significant role in accelerating innovation in critical industries. Da Rin and Penas[6] argue that VC helps in building the absorptive capacity that is much needed in most industries. In research carried out by Da Rin and Penas (that compared the effects of public-funded firms with those provided by private investors),

4 ABC Investments, 'Role of Venture Capital in the Economic Growth of the United States'.
5 Berkeley Economics, 'The Economics of Ideas'.
6 Da Rin and Penas, 'The Effect of Venture Capital on Innovation Strategies'.

it was found out that the capitalists are always very careful with their capital. This makes these venture capitalists venture into the industries that have more potential growth. The venture capitalists do not only provide capital to the businesses but also some advice and expertise to the companies they invest in. The companies are also made to engage in innovation activities that lead to accumulation of the absorptive capacity and in research and development projects. Researching investment in a certain field does not only help the firm to avoid making losses but also help in the formulation of strategic plans that can be used to offer a conducive environment for innovation to take place. For companies operating under public funding, there are no services such as management and advice, and the investors leave the management to make their own decisions after the fund has been provided. Lack of strategic guidance hinders innovations in such companies[7]. To add on that, the venture capitalist may also bring an expert in a certain field to evaluate the prevailing problems and come up with the best solution to address it.

Third, VC has a significant impact on the micro-level of the economy. At this level, the venture capitalists undertake two main activities to the companies they invest in: they provide capital and add value to them. Provision of money for start-up and growth is the main objective of the VC. Most of the companies and individuals fail to reach out their full potential and achieve their targets simply because they lack capital and advice to help them maximize their operations and strategies. The fear of being left alone in the management of the business has also been a limiting factor to the companies and individuals. However, the approach of the VC comes as a surprise to most businesses as the venture capitalists engage their partners to ensure that they are fully equipped with the necessary information in financial matters and guidance they may need when carrying out their activities. Although financial institutions may provide capital to

7 Da Rin and Penas, 'The Effect of Venture Capital on Innovation Strategies'.

the local business, they lack incentives that encourage enterprises to opt for their option.[8]

At the first stages of investment, the capitalists provide funds and expertise to the companies, which are the most important components in investments and therefore adding value to the portfolio companies. However, the approach used by the venture capitalists will vary from one company to another. According to Gadiesh and MacArthur,[9] there are five main principles that the private investors or venture capitalists apply in their operations: acceleration of performance in the industries, harnessing of talent from the local market, elimination of underperforming and unproductive capital for creating space for other ventures, fostering a result-oriented mindset and the definition of full potential.

The venture capitalists not only invest their money during the administration phase but also the activities of the pre-investment phase and exit. This ensures that the value of the company is constant, and resources are always available when needed. Furthermore, there are various ways in which the venture capitalists can add value to the company where they invest which includes promoting the expert behaviour of the company, making timely decisions based on the market conditions, adopting improved policies of human resource management among others.[10]

According to Ueda and Hirukawa,[11] the effects of VC are context specific which depends on variables such as the phase of the project, the source of innovation and the type of venture and portfolio companies. Therefore, the impact of these ventures is not uniform in all industries. For example, VC may have more impact on the

---

8 Senor and Singer, *Start-up Nation*.
9 Gadiesh and MacArthur, *Lessons from Private Equity Any Company Can Use*.
10 Lockett et al., 'The Export Intensity of Venture Capital-backed Companies', 39–58.
11 Ueda and Hirukawa, 'Venture Capital and Productivity'.

innovations in the manufacturing industry as compared to the agricultural industry. Furthermore, when the VC companies are investing, they consider the nature of the host country. In a developing country, the venture capitalists tend to invest mostly in agriculture as it is the main sector of the most Third-World economies.

In India, VC was initiated by the government and financial institutions. As compared to the rest of the world where the capital investors are private entrepreneurs who provide funds, mentoring and guidance to the entrepreneurs, the Indian capital investors used to be large financial institutions which could only provide capital to the firms. However, over a period, the government realized that this approach was not working in the country, although it was successful in western nations. The government changed its policies to restore the confidence in start-ups by allowing private investors into the deal. The success of the country in the information technology was enough evidence that there was a potential investment opportunity in the knowledge-based industries.[12] However, the potential growth was not limited in one industry but also relevant in many areas such as telecommunication, agriculture, food processing and services among others. Since then, the VC has been of great importance to the Indian economy, especially to the start-ups.

To begin with, VC bridges the gap where the traditional sources of capital, such as the financial institutions cannot fund the new venture. Through VC, the Indians in various industries have been able to get management support and smart advice through private investors. The main reason that makes them offer these services is to protect their capital against risks that may come as a result of poor management. To add on that, these services have played a role, and VC has helped many start-ups to turn their vision into a marketable product. Through the market venture, the Indian government has

12 IHS Global Insight, *Venture Impact*.

also been able to protect the local business environment as well as its entrepreneurs who are vulnerable to multinationals.

Second, VC has helped in improving the quality of goods and services in the country. The capitalists provide funds, expertise and service to the start-ups as well other enterprises that show potential growth. The availability of expertise and better management in certain industries have made the number of firms to increase significantly. The rise in the number of firms also means that there will be stiff competition in the market as every company is trying to sell off their products. To gain a competitive advantage in the market, firms have to come up with smart and effective strategies. However, one of the default strategies that the majority of the firms tend to implement is to improve the quality of their goods and services so that they can win the trust of the customers in the market. As a result, the overall quality of goods and services in certain industries are improved as everyone is trying to win a bigger market share.

Finally, VC has enabled local companies to expand. The capital invested is used in creating more branches as the companies are looking to increase its operations in the industry. The ability to expand the enterprise also means that the firm can be able to create more employment for the local population. As one of the countries with the highest rate of unemployment in Asia (6.1%), the VC has played a significant role in trying to reduce the unemployment rate in the country.[13] Furthermore, creating employment for the citizens is one of the goals that the government aims to achieve shortly. To add on that, a good number of VC companies in India such as the Nexus Venture Partners, SEE Fund, Blume Venture Advisors, etc., have enjoyed much success in their respective industries. Their growth has been a result of the fund management and expertise provided by VC firms. The VC-backed companies have greatly contributed to the

13 ET Bureau, 'Is the Job Scene in India Bad? Depends on How You See It, Says Govt'.

growth of the economy in the country through the inflow of capital into the country. The firms have created a considerable number of employment vacancies to the locals. The venture-backed companies are also engaging in other corporate social responsibilities activities such as the building of social amenities such as schools and hospitals as well as offering scholarship opportunities to students in the country. In addition to above mentioned activities, increase in operations in the country increases the tax base of the country, and therefore increasing the revenue of the government. Therefore, the importance of venture in the Indian economy cannot be overlooked.

KEY VC PLAYERS AND KEY DEALS

The key VC players in India include Accel Partners, India Quotient, Saama Capital, Matrix Partners, Lightspeed India Partners, ICICI Venture, SAIF Partners, DSG Consumer Partners, Sequoia Capital India Advisors, Blume Ventures, Inventus Capital Partners India, Chiratae Ventures, Kalaari Capital, Matrix Partners, Omnivore Partners, Helion Venture Partners, Jungle Ventures, Kae Capital, Infuse Ventures, SIDBI Venture Capital and Khosla Ventures.

Nexus Venture Partners and Snapdeal

The Nexus Venture Partners is one of the largest homegrown investment capital firms in India. Nexus Venture Partners has made around seven investments, all in start-ups with early-stage or growth-stage phase in both the USA and India. The firm has categorized its funding strategy where it invests from $500,000 to $10 million in start-ups with early-stage or growth-stage phases. The firm makes an investment of $500,000 through its seed programs. It invests in a wide range of industries such as data security, infrastructure, Internet, outsources services, energy, consumer and business services, mobile, big data analytics, cloud storage, the rural sector, agribusiness, media and technology. The firm has invested in various Indian start-ups such as Delhivery, PubMatic, ScaleArc, Komli, Housing and Snapdeal.

In the initial days of Snapdeal, Nexus Venture Partners invested in the company in 2010. The company invested $22 million in Snapdeal and has, over the years, invested a total of around $45 million in different rounds. The investment of the firm reached its peak in 2016 when it reached a value of over $6.5 billion. After reaching its peak valuation for the investment, the firm has not gained much out of this investment in the start-up. The reason for this can be the use of strategies that have not played well for the venture capitalist firm.

Nexus Venture Partners has around $1.2 billion assets under management, and the firm is continuously involved in raising funds for new start-ups and raised $450 million in 2015.[14] Founded in February 2010, Snapdeal is an e-commerce firm operating in India. The company operates in the same industry as Flipkart does. It has over 300,000 sellers and over 800 categories with over 30 million products. The company operates all across the country, connecting a vast consumer base to an enormous seller base. Over the years, the company has managed to acquire various small businesses to increase its reach and growth in the market. Most of the company's acquisitions were in 2015, which includes its acquisition of Smartprix, Exclusively, Gojavas and various others.

In 2016, the company went for a merger with its rival Flipkart, for which the process continued till mid of 2017. Snapdeal intended to merge with Flipkart with a value of $1 billion. However, in July 2017, the merger deal failed to get full approval of all the investors. The majority of the initial investors of Snapdeal were responsible for the failure of the deal related to the merger. The management of Snapdeal decided to move ahead independently and was backed by

14 Chanchani, 'Nexus Venture Partners Eyes $400 million in Fifth Fund'.

its board of directors in decision of following independent path. The management of Snapdeal believed that India's 200 billion market is yet to be explored by the e-commerce players and so moving Snapdeal into future independently will bear better returns. Also, the investors of Snapdeal were reluctant of merger with Flipkart because of tax issues that will emerge for the investors of Snapdeal post-merger. This merger would create a tax liability of millions of dollars for investors of Snapdeal. However, during this time, the company sold its previously acquired company FreeCharge, which is a mobile payment platform in $60 million to Axis Bank at a loss as it was acquired at the cost of $400 million. The company has faced various issues as well, including labour issues, where the allegations on the company were that it was forcefully firing employees. These allegations led to the government ordering the labour department of the country to probe the accusations.

IDG Ventures and Yatra

The IDG Ventures has been among the top venture capitalist firms to invest in Indian start-ups. The company has made various investments in several start-ups ranging from industry to industry. It is a leading technology-focused VC funding firm, which specializes in funding promising start-ups from early to expansion stages. The investment range that the company has for start-ups is from $1 million to $10 million depending on the business, nature and market evaluation. Engineering, enterprise software, digital consumers are various industries where the company has invested. Some of the start-ups funded by the company are Myntra, Zivame, Ozone Media, iProf, FirstCry, UNBXD and Yatra.[15]

In 2014, Yatra raised $23 million in funding from IDG Ventures. Yatra aimed to increase the growth speed of the company from the

15 Inc42, 'Top 47 Most Active Venture Capital Firms in India for Startups'.

investment received.[16] IDG Ventures has invested in Yatra in three rounds of funding from its inception to the current time. The reason for the investment by IDG Ventures in Yatra was because the latter has achieved market leadership in attracting more domestic hotels along with attractive packages segment that can help them attract more consumers. In 2011, Yatra further raised a funding of $2 billion from various investors, including Norwest Venture Partners, Valiant Capital Management and IDG Ventures. Founded in 2006, Yatra is an Indian firm operating as a travel search engine and online travel agency. The company has grown with ups and downs over the years. In 2012, it managed to reach the second spot in India for online travel services. It acquired around 30 per cent of the market share with a valuation of $5.4 billion. The company is competing with several competitors in India such as Expedia, Via, Goibibo, Cleartrip and MakeMyTrip. Yatra offers reservation facilities in over 12,000 hotels across India and over 400,000 globally. The company offers holiday packages over 5,000 and 20,000 tickets daily.[17] From the time of its inception, Yatra has made some acquisitions to grow, which includes Travel Services International, which was a ticked consolidator in 2010, MagicRooms, which was a global distribution system offering firm and Buzzintown, which was an Indian entertainment and event portal. It further acquired Travelguru in 2012 by gaining 100 per cent stake in the firm. It further acquired Travel-logs in 2016, which is specialized in customized private tours and city walks.[18] With various rounds of funding to achieve market growth and success, Yatra has managed to receive $88 million in funding. The company has increased its reach by either acquiring smaller firms that were

16 Abudheen, 'Yatra.com Raises $23M in a New Round from IDG Ventures and Temasek's VC Arm Vertex'.
17 Ibid.
18 Abudheen, 'Yatra.com Raises $23M in a New Round from IDG Ventures and Temasek's VC Arm Vertex'.

aligned with the objectives of the company or by improving the services it offers to the consumers.[19]

Sequoia Capital India and Justdial

Sequoia Capital India is among the top companies looking for investing in start-ups. The company specializes in seeding start-ups, be it in the early, mid or late phases. It aims for public expanding and growth-stage firms. The company invests from $100,000 to $1 million in start-ups with seed-stage phase. The investing goes higher from $1 million to $10 million for start-ups with the early-stage phase. It further goes up from $10 million to $100 million for start-ups with the growth-stage phase. The company has invested in various small ventures such as DailyNinja, a Bengaluru-based delivery start-up, Raw Pressery, which is a Mumbai-based organic juice start-up, Justdial and various others.

The Sequoia Capital India has invested over $55 million in Justdial. In 2009, the company, along with the VC companies Tiger Global and SAIF partners, invested ₹164.4 million in Justdial. In addition to this, the company invested ₹600 million, followed by third investment in Justdial for around ₹3,050 million. The funding in the latter went for three rounds of investment from Sequoia Capital India and other VC firms. The investment made by Sequoia Capital India in Justdial led to the former holding over 5 per cent of shares in the latter. Justdial is an Indian firm that offers local search services to a variety of other services online and over the phone. It was founded in 1996 by V. S. S. Mani, and the company has grown over the years. It has its offices all across the country and employs around 13,000 employees and has an existing database of over 25 million listings. It also has active paid campaigns for over 500,000. Justdial went

19 Ibid.

public in 2013 by offering over 13.5 million shares to the public from its 17.5 million shares.[20] The rest of the shares were given to the 15 investors of the company. Apart from the listing of different service numbers, the company also offers Justdial Social, which is a service aimed to aggregate content from a TV broadcast, social media websites, news and various other sources. It also has another service named Search Plus Services, which manages all the online transactions using mobile apps and web. Currently, the venture capitalist firm Sequoia Capital India is on the path of exiting Justdial. The company has sold a huge amount of its shares in the open market. As per the Bombay Stock Exchange (BSE) filing, the firm used to hold over 5 per cent stake in Justdial, and with the selling of over 600,000 shares, which represented around 1 per cent of the company, it has reduced its shares count in the company. The shares of Sequoia Capital India are reduced from 5.17 per cent to 2.18 per cent. Sequoia Capital India sold its shares to HDFC Mutual Fund.[21] On the other hand, Justdial has managed to grow its market size and profit over the years.

Inventus Capital Partners and Policybazaar

Inventus Capital Partners has the sole aim of backing new entrepreneurs and making them successful. This VC is managed by industry-operating veterans and entrepreneurs with the knowledge of investments. The company is a US-India-based firm and invests in start-ups in both India and the USA. In India, it manages over ₹8,000 million in three different funds.

Inventus has backed various companies over the years, specifically seeking capital-related opportunities in technologically affiliated companies. Inventus Capital Partners has invested in Insta Health,

20 Susmit, 'Sequoia Capital Sells Just Dial Stake Worth ₹51.56 crore'.
21 KJ, 'Sequoia Capital Sheds Further 5% Stake in JustDial for ₹135 crore'.

Power2SME, Lemnisk, Savaari, eDreams, HealthifyMe, MoveInSync, Tricog, Truebil, redBus, Sokrati, FundsIndia, Cbazaar, Policybazaar, UNBXD, Peel-Works, Aasaanjobs, KNOLSKAPE.[22] From the time of its inception in 2008, Policybazaar has managed to go for seven rounds of funding and so far, has raised over $366 million. Inventus Capital Partners, one of the primary investors in the company, along with Intel Capital, invested $9 million in series A investment funding round. In its third round of funding, Policybazaar further raised $20 million from its previous investor Inventus Capital Partners and Tiger Global Management. Various other investors have also invested in the firm from time to time in its seven round of funding. In 2018, the company raised $238 million in its existing last round of funding where SoftBank Group invested $150 million in the company and gained 15 per cent of stake in Policybazaar's parent company ETechAces Marketing and Consulting.

Policybazaar is an Indian start-up founded in 2008. It is involved in the business of insurance and works as an insurance aggregator and a technological, financial firm. In addition to this, the firm also offers its services through digital platforms such as apps and websites.[23] Users can compare various financial services from different insurance companies. Following the success of its growth in the country, the firm has also expanded its business in the international market, starting from the United Arab Emirates. Policybazaar has made changes to its business strategy from time to time. Where it used to only offer information and price comparison of insurance policies of different insurance companies, now it has started to offer and selling insurance products as well.

Policybazaar has processed around 25 per cent of life insurance in India and covers around 7 per cent of the retail health cover in

22 Policybazaar.com, 'Our Investors'.
23 Gooptu, 'Policybazaar Raises $5 million from Inventus Capital, Info Edge and Intel Capital'.

India. The company offers all types of insurance-related plans, such as motor insurance, health insurance, travel insurance and life insurance. The company depended on lead generation as the primary source of revenue, which contributed to around 85 per cent of the company's revenue until 2011. At present, with the introduction of different revenue sources, the company earns around 85 per cent of its revenue from policy sales and e-commerce. The company's turnover increased by over 225 per cent in 2018. With the latest funding and investments made in the company by Info Edge and SoftBank, the valuation of the company has increased and reached more than $1 billion.[24]

Accel Partners and Flipkart

The Accel Partners has long been one of the major venture capitalists for Indian start-ups. The company, based in the USA and Bengaluru, has funded various companies such as Flipkart, Myntra, Komli, Yepme and various others. Accel Partners invests from $500,000 to $50 million in start-up companies and the industries receiving investment are highly diverse. It includes infrastructure, mobile and software, Internet and consumer services, cloud-enabled services and various others.

The company seeded Flipkart with $800,000 back in 2008, when the latter was starting a never before journey in the country. Accel further invested over $100 million in the e-commerce company. The reason for Accel to fund Flipkart was the initial stage where the e-commerce market was still new to India, and with big players such as Sequoia Capital, who passed the opportunity to invest in Flipkart, Accel grabbed the opportunity. The funding was not an easy feat to achieve as back in 2008, and it was not easy to evaluate the sheer scale of what this e-commerce platform can offer a decade later.

24 Kumar, 'PolicyBazaar - Story, Founder, Business Model, Funding, Team, News'.

The Accel Partners funded Flipkart in the latter's initial days, and all the funding was not achieved in a single round. Over the years, Accel has managed to invest in the e-commerce giant by investing money from time to time. Accel's focus is always on the initial round of funding, which is the primary reason it seeded and funded the series A funding in the e-commerce company.[25] After the first round of funding, the company invested the second time after 21 months, considering the growth Flipkart was achieving. Accel invested $1 million in 2009 in Flipkart, which has now valued over $15.2 billion. Flipkart is one of the two largest e-commerce giants in the country and has come a long way from its initial days. This Bengaluru-based firm has managed to overcome various challenges and sustained competition from the global giant Amazon in the country. Flipkart is the reason for both pioneering and introducing e-commerce in the Indian market. Apart from a wide range of products, the company has also managed to develop its own logistics centres in the country in addition to the delivery fleets. All this combined help the company in delivering high quality and end-to-end experience to both the consumers and the sellers.

At present, the company has over 33,000 employees all across the offices in the country, and the company offers over 33 million products from its more than 70 categories. Along with serving a huge consumer base, it also serves over 50 million shoppers on an annual basis and is constantly becoming a quickly growing e-commerce player in the country. The company managed to raise over $3.2 billion for its growth and expansion efforts from different investment firms.[26] Recently, it was acquired by the US giant Walmart to compete with Amazon in India, which has also slowly led to Accel reducing its shareholding in the e-commerce giant. In 2017, the company completed 10 years of its existence and successful growth. Kalyan

25 Chanchani, 'Flipkart Investor Accel Raises $450 million for Fifth India Fund'.
26 Accel, 'Flipkart'.

Krishnamurthy was named the new CEO of the company, and its mobile wallet payment system crossed over 10 million user base. The company also raised over $1.4 billion from eBay, Tencent and Microsoft and managed to make eBay India a part of the Flipkart group. In the same year, SoftBank invested in the company and became one of the shareholders with the largest company shares.

4

WHAT DOES VENTURE CAPITALIST LOOK FOR IN AN INVESTMENT?

With the deal still in infant stage, there is no financial data available to understand the mechanics of the deal. Deeper we go into the deal, it becomes more complex to value it and the criteria becomes more subjective. In the early stage of the deal, a lot is about subjectivity. However, it still requires to be evaluated with quantitative numbers. The criteria in the early stage tend to be less about company financials and more about people running the business (promoters), past experience of the business and the market reputation of promoters. The other part of the deal is as to how attractive is the industry. For example, a company in steel industry cannot generate enormous margins as these margins are driven by the nature of the industry in which the company operates. The nature of the industry and company's performance both drive the margins and company alone cannot change it. So, the industry plays a crucial role in the selection of a portfolio company for an investment. The venture capitalists choose to invest in an industry where enormous margins can be created and where the return on invested capital (ROIC) can be huge. Also, the industry requires lesser capital investment to build products that can generate exponential returns. The venture capitalist work on expanding the business without focusing on profitability as research shows that once the scale becomes too big, it is easier to generate profitability.

As VC is a form of equity financing, the entrepreneurs would not have to face the same burden that they would have faced in the case of borrowing a loan from a financial institute. This would help them to focus on the growth and expansion of the business, which would generate better returns, as they would not have to worry about paying back the money along with interest after a specific period.

Numerous businesses are started every year across the globe. If investors start investing in each business that they come across, they will lose more than what they would gain through the returns. Before investing in any of these businesses or start-ups, they must evaluate them. The evaluation process can vary from industry to industry depending on the business type.[1] It is essential to evaluate the business so that the investor can understand the cost and benefit of the investment.

In the initial stage of a business, there is not any financial data that can be used to assess the opportunity of investing in it. This is a significant issue when it comes to evaluating the deal of investing in a new start-up, as compared to existing businesses that are in their middle stage or maturity stages. In the initial stage of the business, the deal is very subjective as discussed above. For instance, what might seem like an opportunity to the entrepreneurs might not seem the same to the investors. This chapter will focus on the individuals running a new venture and their experiences as compared to the venture's financial information.

Along with this, the strengths and weaknesses of the business, competitors and their reputation in the market are assessed. All this information is necessary for a venture capitalist before the decision of investment is made. Overall, five main factors play a crucial role in helping venture capitalist decide on whether to invest in a business or not. These five factors include opportunities in the market, competitive edge, team, uniqueness and deal characteristics (Figure 4.1).

1 Camp, *Venture Capital Due Diligence*.

Figure 4.1 Deal Evaluation

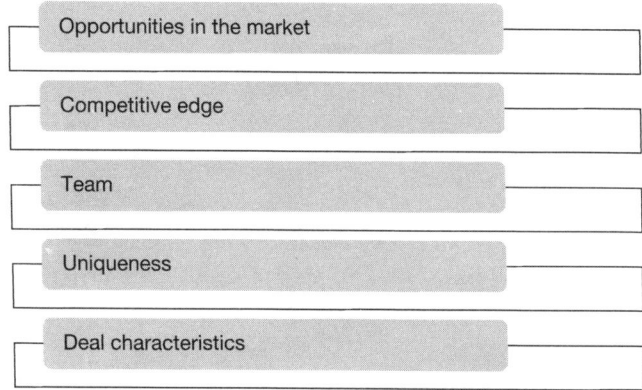

Opportunities in the market

Competitive edge

Team

Uniqueness

Deal characteristics

OPPORTUNITIES IN THE MARKET

Different markets offer different levels of opportunities to the businesses operating in it. For businesses to be successful, they must conduct research of the market. The information obtained through this is what the investors would be interested in knowing and evaluating whether the business would have any worth in the market or not. Understanding the nature of the market that the business will be operating in would benefit the entrepreneurs, as well as the venture capitalists, to determine the sort of expertise it would be requiring. Certain aspects that the investors would be interested in knowing are mentioned here (Figure 4.2).

Percentage of the Entire Market

To have an understanding of the market share that the business might makeup, it is necessary to know what the entire market looks like, what it comprises and if there is any room for new businesses in it or not. The overall size of a market and its percentage provides the entrepreneur as well as the investors with much information that

Figure 4.2 Opportunities in the Market

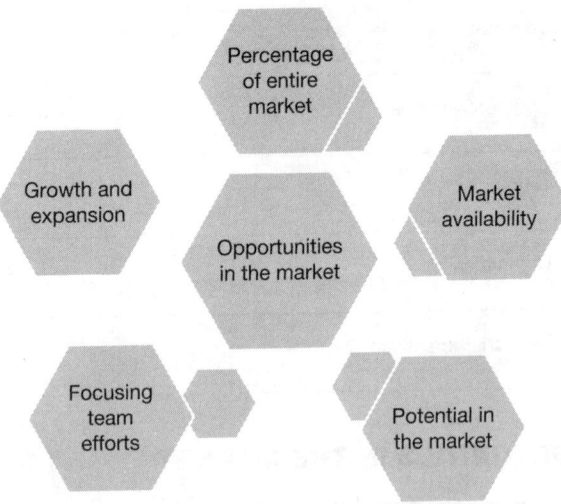

can be used for various decisions. The first thing that the size and percentage of the market explain is the sales of the market and the share in the overall industry earned by each company operating for a specific time. This information provides an overall idea about the market and the competitor operating in it. This helps the new businesses know who they are going to compete against and if they have the necessary resources for competing against various businesses. This information is beneficial for investors and venture capitalists to determine if the company would be able to take a position for itself.

Market Availability

The percentage of the market that is available to be served by the business is another aspect that should be taken into consideration. For instance, it would not make sense for an entrepreneur to enter into a market that is already very saturated, as it would be difficult to make a place for themselves. Thus, the entrepreneur should know whether there is a place in the market for the business and products or not. Numerous markets are very lucrative, but at the same time, they are saturated and have huge competitors. For instance, the market for carbonated drinks such as Coca-Cola and Pepsi is not an ideal option. Unless the entrepreneur has something unique to offer, venture capitalists would not even consider such business ideas for investment. Entrepreneurs and businesses need to identify the place that they can make for themselves in the market, as well as ensure that they would be able to capitalize on it.

Potential in the Market

While analysing the market and determining whether it would be profitable enough to enter or not, the entrepreneurs must examine the potential target market and the potential buyers. There are different buyers within the same target market, and it is the responsibility of the business to determine the customer segment to target in order to maximize its profits. Every individual is looking for something unique even in the most generic products, and this is what differentiates the buyers with the same target market. The entrepreneur and the management need to examine the potential within the market before they decide to enter it. This is not something that should be left for the last minute. Businesses can no longer expect that the product they develop or want to sell would attract customers for no reason. Although if the product is unique and one of its kind, the business can start by creating a need and attracting the customers, but even then, it would need to have some potential buyers.

Focusing Team Efforts

The sector on which the team focusses its efforts helps the business determine where to launch the product and how to do so. The product needs to be launched in an area where the customers would be willing to pay for it. It depends on the efforts and the focus of the team when it comes to ensuring whether the business would be a success or not. Solely focusing on one aspect of the market or operations would not help the company in the long run to achieve its goals and objectives. Instead, the team should have an understanding of all this and try to focus on all the aspects of the business that would benefit them and ensure the profitability of the business.

Growth and Expansion

The market that the business wants to enter should have opportunities for growth and expansion. Entering a market that does not have any possibilities for future expansion and growth can eventually become a dead weight.[2] Not only would it drown the investments, but it would also be difficult for the business to become sustainable in the long run. Businesses today need to answer that they can grow and develop as the company matures. It should not be the case where the entrepreneur would have to shut the business down once it matures. Providing such information would take the investors into confidence that the managers and the entrepreneur are focused on running the business for the long run instead of merely trying their luck at a business to which they would not even give their full focus and time.

COMPETITIVE EDGE

The competitive edge in a given organization is defined by its business model which in turn is governed by factors including sources of revenue, business strategy, target customer, pricing strategy and supply chain. Every organization has a specific business model that the management or a person they have hired or kept, develops to help the organization with starting up the business. An entrepreneur

---

2 Samila and Sorenson, 'Venture Capital, Entrepreneurship, and Economic Growth'.

needs to have an understanding of the business model that he wants to implement and should have a thorough framework that can be shared with investors on demand. The business model of the start-up is just as relevant for the venture capitalists in determining whether to invest in the business or not, as the company overview is. Although the two might seem like the same thing, they cover very different information. Some of the information that should be included in this model is discussed here.

Although the primary source of revenue generation would be the product or service being sold, along with this, there could be other sources of revenue that would help with the running and maintenance expenses of the organization as well. Having more than a single source of revenue would help the business stay afloat in case the market for one slows up. However, before deciding on something like this, the cost analysis of both revenue sources should be carried out, along with ensuring that the products or service would be developed from similar if not the same raw material. Selling and finding a use for the by-products does not only reduce waste, but it is a profitable method for developing an additional source of revenue for the business.

The overall business strategy that will be implemented across the organization determines the number of different aspects about the organization. It comprises a set of decisions or actions that will help the entrepreneur in accomplishing the goals and objectives of the business. It is the overall framework of a plan that the company will be implementing to ensure that it has a strong and competitive standing within the market, a smooth operation of the activities, satisfy customers and accomplish the desired goals and objectives. It is a long-term sketch of what the business will be doing, how it will be doing that and what are the expected outcomes of the activities. It provides the company with a sense of direction and a destination. Without an efficient and effective strategy, the company would be unable to achieve its desired results. This is something that the VC would be interested in knowing, as the business strategy is the starting point for any business and should be strong and efficient.

The target customer segment to market the product or service is another crucial aspect of the business model of the start-up. As already mentioned, this information would help the business by determining the number of strategies and decisions that will be implemented. Identifying the target customer would help the business with determining the price point, the method of promotion and placement of the product. For instance, it would not make sense to market junk food to health-conscious people. Organizations must determine the customer segment as it would help in establishing the overall marketing strategies that the business would be incorporating. Businesses that do not know their customers are unable to satisfy their needs or develop a business that would be successful in the long run.

The pricing strategy that the organization will follow would play a vital role in determining various marketing strategies. There are a number of different pricing strategies that the business can incorporate and benefit from. Before determining the strategy and the price that the business will charge its consumers, the firm must understand who the consumers are and how the firm wants to brand and market its product. The pricing strategy and the price being charged to the consumer will help the venture capitalists in understanding whether the business plans are penetrating the market or skimming through it. This sort of strategy would help investors understand several things about the company such as its intended consumer market and its profit generation plans. Having a well-sought pricing strategy depends a lot on the product being offered and who it is being offered to.

A thorough overview of the supply chain of the organization should be provided to the venture capitalists. The supply chain of an organization is the network of resources, individuals and organizations that help the business from sourcing raw materials to making them available to the consumers at the end of the chain. The models of supply chain vary across industries and much depend on the type of business and its consumers. Some businesses have a short supply chain, while others have a very detailed and complex supply chain. It is the size of the organization that determines its suppliers and distributors and the other middlemen. This information would help the venture capitalists in understanding whether the entrepreneur has determined the model through which it would be procuring the raw material, converting it to finished products, storing it and then delivering it to the consumers.

TEAM

The human resource that makes up the organization at all the different levels play a vital role in the existence of the organization. The entrepreneurs cannot run a business without having efficient and productive members of their team. This is why it is necessary to have a list off all the talented people who will take up the strategic positions within the firm. Apart from highlighting and discussing the experts and managers that will be managing and directing the firm, an overview of the overall employees should also be provided to the investors. All this information should be available to the venture capitalists. Necessary human resource aspects are discussed in detail in the following pages.

Although the human resource at any level of the organization plays an important role, the top management of the organization is of immense importance for several reasons. It is the top management of any organization that leads the company towards success and makes the necessary decisions to guide the firm and provide it with vital skills and knowledge. By having energetic, skilful, knowledgeable and capable top management, the organization would not only be able to make effective and robust strategies that would be beneficial both in short and long run but also it would attract the investors towards the business. Venture capitalists are mostly interested in the individuals who make up the top management of the organization, as it would provide them with the necessary information regarding the abilities and capabilities of the firm. Thus, the entrepreneur should have the ability and capacity to source and headhunt individuals who would be an asset for the organization.

Apart from the top management of the business, the entrepreneur should also source and bring on board advisors who are known for their roles. These individuals acting as board members would provide the necessary information and guidance with regards to operational activities of the company. These individuals are not mandatory for the business, but are a strong team of advisors who would convince the investors that they are making the right decisions by investing in a particular business. Such individuals can complement the skills and abilities of the top management and ensure that the company is on the right path, and they would provide the top management with insight that would make the business profitable. Along with this, these individuals can be beneficial in sourcing members for the top management of the organization as well. While venture capitalists do provide firms and new start-ups with necessary information about running a successful business, having qualified advisors on the team would put them at ease as well.

The entrepreneur would not hire and select people for the aforementioned positions randomly, instead he/she would have to carry out a need analysis for these positions and only then hire people to fill them in. The need analysis is not only carried out for administrative but also for financial purposes. Since most of the new start-ups have a minimal source of funds, they cannot hire experts and top management on a whim. Instead, these individuals are hired after thoroughly evaluating the positions and determining the need for them. While having a strong pool of top management and advisors is beneficial for the organization, it should be able to justify each individual that is brought on board and how the firm would benefit from their presence. Simply hiring individuals because they have a positive image and various skills is not enough. Instead, the firm should have the necessary information to provide the VCs with so that the sources of the company can be evaluated thoroughly.

While having a strong pool of internal human resource is necessary, it is of similar significance for the business to identify and develop relationships with external partners as well. A firm would have to deal with various other companies and individuals across the supply chain. Apart from the supply chain, the company should also identify other partners and organizations that it would benefit from, so it can develop beneficial relationships. These individuals and companies can play a vital role in the operational effectiveness of the start-up. Therefore, it is necessary to identify them and provide an overview of them to the venture capitalists when discussing the deal with them.

Finally, an overview of the expertise that the team has, specifically the top management, should be discussed in the information being provided to the venture capitalists. Having experienced and qualified individuals on the team would highlight the potential and capabilities of the start-up. Each individual is unique and would offer a unique set of skills. However, it is their collective abilities which would set them apart from other firms and businesses requiring funding. All this information would make it beneficial for the investors to know the worth of the soft skills that the organization possesses. This way, they would be better able to determine the worth of the prospective organization.

UNIQUENESS

Whenever a new business idea is introduced to the market, sooner or later, other entrepreneurs and organizations step into the market as well. By and large, almost every product and service that are provided in the market has a competitor in some form, whether a direct or an indirect competitor. Thus, before stepping into a new business or market, the entrepreneur must evaluate the competitive landscape of the market. By doing so, the management of the business would have a better understanding of the returns and revenue that would be generated from the product or services being offered. Along with this, it would help the company in underrating what it can do differently to attract new customers and to make a loyal customer base for itself. Some of the significant aspects regarding competitive landscape will be discussed in the following pages.

Setting up a business might seem like an easy task, but it is not. Individuals cannot only decide to open up a business somewhere and go along with the idea. Not only because it would have to follow through specific regulations and rules but also because it might not be an easy task to enter specific markets. At times, there are markets that have very strong barriers to entry, which would make it difficult for the business to enter the desired market.[3] Operating in the market might require high capital for setting up the business, which would not make it difficult for entrepreneurs to enter the market, even if it is profitable and lucrative. Along with this, there might be high costs associated with customers shifting from an existing product to a new one.[4] Thus, these barriers need to be examined and understood when entering the market or deciding which market to enter.

The strategies that are being incorporated to compete with existing players are something that any business cannot overlook. There is hardly any market where a business might not have to compete with other businesses. Since the business would be competing for the same role materials, customers and other factors, therefore it is not favourable to only understand how to compete with these competitors effectively. The focus is to develop plans and strategies

3 Geroski and Jacquemin, *Barriers to Entry and Strategic Competition*.
4 Golis, *Enterprise and Venture Capital*.

that would help the management and employees to be better at what they do in comparison to their competitors. There are various tactics and strategies that a company can implement to make themselves more competitive and overpass competitors. Organizations can use various factors to their benefit and can add them to their competitive strategy. This is where the competitive advantage of a company plays a vital role.

There are certain aspects of the business that are unique to it, which can become an advantage for the business over its competition. Through this advantage, what the company is able to offer will be of much better value. It could either mean lower prices, more benefits, or services through which the highly charged prices can be justified.[5] There are different factors that an organization can use as a competitive advantage. It can be a unique raw material, a robust supply chain, excellent relationships with customers, efficient and competent human resources, skilful top management and so on. Once the company identifies its competitive advantage, it should use it to its benefit and ensure that it is sustainable.

If the market is lucrative and has low barriers to entry, it is evident that other players would enter the market as well. The entrepreneur should understand that if he can enter the market, so can other players as well. This is why a new start-up must benefit the most from the opportunities being provided by the market to new entrants. At the same time, it should try to differentiate itself and its services with products from other businesses, so that it can retain its position and continue to attract new customers while retaining the existing ones.[6]

When a business develops new product and presents it in the market, it usually gets the benefit of being an early bird. The organization and its management must understand the benefit of this and how it

5 Gerken and Whittaker, *The Little Book of Venture Capital Investing*; Geroski and Jacquemin, *Barriers to Entry and Strategic Competition*.
6 Klonowski, *The Venture Capital Investment Process*.

can take advantage of these benefits.[7] This is something that can be observed in the tech industry. Organizations that are the first ones to come up with new technology are usually the ones to get the most out of it. Thus, they need to invest their time and resources in developing a product which would provide them with this leverage.

Although it is not an easy task to do so or even a preferable one, an organization should look for factors that would be incorporated to deter new entrants and existing rivals in the market. This can be something simple and straightforward, such as patenting the product, or it can be a more complex set of strategies and tactics that would deter organizations from entering the market. Although at times, such tactics might be deemed as being passive-aggressive, they can achieve the desired impact. However, this depends on the product and the market to a great extent.

No business can function for very long if it does not have an understanding of its internal environment. Each aspect of the internal environment analysis of a business is essential. It is through this analysis that the company can understand where it stands and what strengths it has, and how these strengths can be incorporated in its daily strategic and tactic activities. These advantages vary from company to company. However, some essential strengths and opportunities that a company might have can include the aspects that have been discussed in the following pages.

The size of the market and the percentage that it can target effectively can act as a strength for the company. If the size of the market is very small and already saturated, it would not be ideal for the company to start up the business there. Entrepreneurs should look for entering markets that would provide them with a profitable return. This can act as a significant strength for the business in the sense that it would have a substantial customer segment that it can target. Also, markets

7 Markides and Geroski, *Fast Second.*

that have a substantial size which tend to have better suppliers, creditors, investors and other partners.

The opportunity to create a good relationship with the customers and attract them to the products and services that are being offered by the company plays as a significant strength for the company. Those organizations that have the understanding and skills for dealing with their customers effectively would also be able to retain them and attract new ones. This is something significant for organizations if they want to develop their customer relationships and become profitable. They need to have customer-centric policies, along with people who understand and implement these policies effectively. This is not something that the companies can overlook.

Having a good and useful business model not only helps the management and other stakeholders to understand what the business is going to do and how it will operate but also it acts as a strength for the organization. Those organizations that have a detailed and well planned out business models know what they want to achieve, and this helps them procure resources and use them effectively and efficiently, to ensure delivery of quality goods and services to the consumers. A thorough business model lays out a thorough framework for the organization, aiding the investors, management and entrepreneurs to be on the same page.

Another aspect of the operations that can become a strength and an opportunity for the business is having strong relationships with various partners in the supply chain. Being able to identify the supply chain partners that would benefit the organization is necessary as it can convert this opportunity into a strength for its operations. There are various partners within a supply chain, who are responsible for fulfilling various operations. By investing time and resources in building strong relationships with these partners, the organization can benefit a lot from it, and it can even become a competitive advantage for the business.

Businesses that are in the manufacturing and assembly business tend to benefit a lot from having efficient and timely production system in place. This would ensure that the products being manufactured are of quality, the organization has an efficient inventory system and that the products are delivered on time to customers. Organizations need to invest in a system that ensures the above, as customers who do not get quality products on time will not return. By developing strategies that would make the production and delivery efficient, it can become a strength for the business, which would benefit it in the long run.

Partnerships in the supply chain are not the only ones that the organization should nurture. Rather, it should focus on partnerships outside the supply chain that would benefit the business in the long run. Relationships with local communities, creditors, investors, competitors and essential business partners should be nurtured and invested in. This would help the business with developing a positive image, positive word of mouth and brand equity. A single partnership can help the organization go a long way and become profitable.

Those organizations that understand the importance of developing a human resource which can act as a competitive advantage for the business tend to go a long way. This is a strength that every organization can benefit from. Human resource and employees are a mandatory part of any organization. Since the organization cannot operate without human resource, it would be beneficial to hire individuals who would become a source of advantage for the organization. Along with hiring the right people, it is also beneficial to train and develop these individuals. An organization with committed, efficient and effective employees operates better than their counterparts with average employees.

Management that has the capacity of adding to the growth and development of the business is a massive strength for the organization. Since the management makes all the strategic decisions, specifically the top management, it is necessary to ensure that the right people are recruited. It can act as a strength for the organization by making the right decisions, attracting necessary funds for the business, developing effective strategies and implementing them at every level of the organization.

While organizations have specific opportunities in the market, which can be converted into strengths, they also have to deal with specific threats and weaknesses. They can come in different forms and sizes. While weaknesses are internal to the organization, threats exist in the external environment. The organizations must identify them and come up with solutions to counter the effects these negative aspects would have on the organization and its operations. Some of the weaknesses and threats that a new start-up might be facing are discussed in the following paragraphs.

As already discussed, the competition in the market has a substantial impact on the organization and its operations. If there are powerful and mature competitors in the market, it can become a threat to the new start-up and its operations. The start-up needs to have a thorough analysis of the market and its competitors to understand how it can compete against them. It would not be impossible to compete with strong competitors, but it would require for them to have effective strategies, all the necessary resources and a strong relationship with various partners. If the start-up is unable to do so, it would be futile to enter a market with mature and robust competitors as they would have a stronghold of the market and the consumers.

If the market has low barriers to entry, it can become another threat, as it makes it easy for everyone to enter the market. With numerous competitors in the market, it would become tough for the organization to capture the attention of the customers and a substantial percentage of the market. Although it would make the market more competitive, and each firm would have to ensure the quality of the product and services, but at the same time it would also mean a decrease in the profit for each firm, specifically for those that operate on a small scale. Thus, the company should consider this when entering a particular market.

In the current age and time, quality of products and services is a significant issue for companies across industries. Consumers are focused on getting value for their money. If one company does not offer quality products and services, they would quickly switch to one that would. Thus, the company should know how to maintain the quality of products and services over a long period. This is not something that should be overlooked or considered secondary by the management, as it would result in a loss of customers, which would mean a decrease in profit for the organization.

Uncertainty in the economic conditions of the country can be a significant issue for organizations at several fronts. First and foremost, it would result in a decrease in the foreign direct investment, which would, in turn, reduce the jobs and the standard of living of the people. This, in turn, means that there would be less income available to be spent on various products. This is not something the organization can control. However, they should have contingency plans that would help the organization to counter such situations and have better opportunities. The conditions of an economy can be predicted, but at the same time, they can change without any precautions.

If there is uncertainty and ambiguity about how success is measured and driven within a market, it will become difficult for organizations to understand where it is standing. This is something where organizations need to develop strategies and metrics to have a better understanding. Such ambiguity would not provide the organization with the necessary information about how to improve its performance and relationship with customers. Organizations would be unable to make it very far if they are unable to know where they stand and what they should be doing to improve their performance.

Fluctuations in the prices of products and services being offered can have a negative impact on the organization and the relationship that it has with its customers. There can be several reasons for this, which are mostly not in the organization's control. The organizations need to understand the reasons behind these fluctuations and try to set a price point which would not have a drastic impact on the buying behaviour of the customers. Factors of demand and supply also have an impact on the prices of the products. Along with this political unrest, natural disasters and the cost of production also impacts the prices of the products. Just like the economic conditions, price fluctuation is something that the companies cannot control, but can learn how to counter and deal with, without having a significant negative impact.

DEAL CHARACTERISTICS

The deal characteristics include company overview as well as the terms and conditions of the deal (Figure 4.3). The first and foremost thing that needs to be done is to understand the organization before a venture capitalist can decide whether to invest in that organization or not. This is an essential aspect of the memo for deal evaluation. The company overview needs to be detailed and thorough so that every aspect of the organization is considered in it.

Figure 4.3 Deal Characteristics

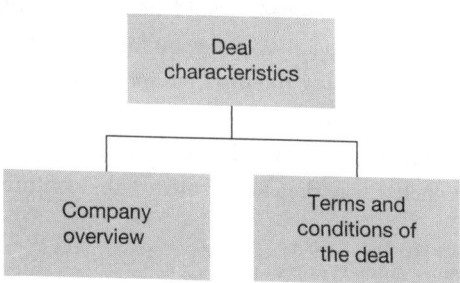

Along with being a description of the business, there should be other necessary information as well. For instance, there should be necessary information about the products and services that the business will be offering to the customers,[8] the benefits of these services to the customers, why it has been developed and what need does it fulfil. The terms and conditions of the deal are one of the most critical aspects of evaluating the deal through which the entrepreneur might get funding for the business. This information is just as important as the various aspects of the organization, its management and the strategies being incorporated. The focus of these terms and conditions are on why the fund is needed and who the entrepreneur will use it for. It is a sort of a justification for the fund that is being asked for by the new start-up. The terms and conditions are not set in isolation, and instead, they depend on the parties involved and the various factors of the business being undertaken. This segment of the paper is focused on the following information.

Company Overview

Any product or service is developed, keeping in mind a specific need of the target segment. Based on the need, the product or service can either be a generic product, a luxury or a niche product. It is necessary for the entrepreneur to clearly explain the purpose of the product or service that it plans on developing and marketing to the consumers. To ensure that the product does fulfil a need of the consumers the business would need to do the necessary research and would need to have relevant information to justify the reasons behind developing the product and deciding to start up a business that would manufacture and sell the product or service.[9] The entrepreneur should have all the necessary information and present it in such a way that would attract the venture capitalists

8 Carver, *Venture Capital Valuation*.
9 Pearce and Barnes, *Raising Venture Capital*.

towards the idea of the business so that they would be willing to invest in it. The purpose of the product should be aligned with the need of the customers as well as the goals and objectives of the business.

The entrepreneur and his team must have an understanding and relevant strategies for the price at which they plan on selling the product or service, how and where it will place the product to ensure the consumer would purchase it, and finally the promotional activities that it will incorporate. While for many organizations, these fours Ps cover up the majority of their marketing strategies in one way or another, this does not mean that these are the only strategies that the start-up should be focusing on. These are just the basic strategies that have a direct impact on the product or service that the business is based on. This information should be discussed in the company overview as well, to provide a general idea of how the company will accomplish the goals and objective from a marketing perspective. There are various strategies that a company would be implementing for each of these aspects, which can only be developed after understanding them.

The focus of businesses today is on being sustainable and eco-friendly, while at the same time being profitable. Thus, the impact the business and its activities would have on the community it operates in should be used for the benefit of the start-up and presented in front of the venture capitalists. This is necessary for investors to know as there might be a possibility for a business to be very lucrative, but at the same time, it might be incorporating activities that would be harmful to the environment and the community. For instance, the start-up might be using raw materials that are either endangered or harmful, making the business unsustainable. Therefore, even if the returns promised are high, the business does not meet the requirement of being sustainable, which is becoming an essential aspect of businesses all over the world.

Finally, the company overview should provide the venture capitalist the information about the problem or an issue that is being solved by the product or service, and how it would impact the various stakeholders, apart from the community and the direct customers. A single business idea can have various impacts on the different stakeholders within the market. Thus, the entrepreneurs must take into consideration the impact that their business would have on the stakeholders. Along with this, they should also aim at improving the relationship with them and focus on having a strong and long-term commitment with them. The effective business has a thorough understanding of their internal as well as external stakeholders, and how they would benefit from the relationships.

The company overview should also discuss the aims, objectives, mission and vision that the founders have. By developing an understanding of what the founders have in mind, the venture capitalists would be able to make a better decision about the importance of the start-up and whether they should invest or not. The entrepreneur should understand the importance of this information, and thus ensure that any unnecessary information is not included in this segment. Unnecessary information might hinder having the desired impact on the investors, as well as miscommunicate the intended information. Along with all this, an overview of who would benefit from the organization should also be presented, if it is not already covered.

Terms and Conditions of the Deal

Amount of Funds

The amount of funds that would be raised through this source of financing is something that should be clearly discussed. The entrepreneur and the VC list should be straightforward about what to expect from one another. The number of funds that the entrepreneur requires should be clearly discussed so that the investors understand whether they can provide that sort of amount of investment or not. This is not something that can be ignored when discussing the terms and conditions of the deal. Instead, it is something around which the whole deal would be based so it should be clearly discussed. The amount that the entrepreneurs have and the amount that it would be borrowed or expected from the venture capitalist to be invested should be at the forefront.[10] If anything is unclear or not specified, then respective parties should reach out and discuss it for clarification. The investors in case of VC would only be paid back in case of an IPO, a merger or an acquisition. Thus, the entrepreneurs would not have to take out cash that could have been used for other aspects of the business.

Purpose of Funds

An entrepreneur should be particular about the purpose of the funds, why the business is reaching out to venture capitalists for a source of funding and how it will be used. This information would develop a sense of transparency between the entrepreneur and venture capitalists, ensuring the latter that their funds are not being misused or misappropriated. If the investors are not provided with the relevant information about the purpose and uses of the investment, it will make it difficult for the general partners to justify the investment to the LPs. Whether the business would use the funds for buying assets, raw materials, setting up a plant or any other purpose, a clear financial justification should be provided to the investors.

Necessary Capital

The amount of working capital and runaway capital that the business has and would need should be discussed and explained as well. This information would provide the investors with the necessary

10 Pearce and Barnes, *Raising Venture Capital*.

numbers, that would show that the management has done its work and understand where and how their capital will be used. Having a substantial amount of working capital would ensure that the business has the opportunity for more investment and growth. Using its own capital for further investment in the business would make it easy for the business to operate over a long time, as it would not have to rely on investment and to borrow more than it should. Having a low level of working and runaway capital would make even basic operations for the business very difficult.

Record Ownership

The entrepreneur should be able to provide the investors with a basic and to the point overview of the record of ownership. This information should include the percentage of ownership that the founders and investors have in the business, dilution of the equity, and value that equity would have in each of the investment rounds. The formation should provide all the details about the investors, the sources of investment and the owners of the business. Managing this information would be beneficial for the investors as well as the owners as they share the equity with ease.

Along with this, such information is beneficial when the business plans on expanding and growing. The general partners would benefit from this information a lot, as they would be able to provide the facts and figures to the LPs if they ever ask for it. Along with this, it would help in calculating the return and profit on the investment quickly at any time.

Burn Rate

The impact that the funding would have on the monthly cash burn is something that should be looked into and shared with the investors as well. The burn rate of any company is the speed at which it would be using up the investment from the VC, to pay for the overhead and operational expenses, before any cash flow can be generated. The rate is mostly estimated as the amount of cash that is spent every month. For instance, if the company has estimated to have a burn rate of $5 million, it means that every month it would be spending an amount of $5 million. This rate is used by both the VC and the start-up firm to keep track of the monthly cash flow before it can generate any income.

5 VALUATION OF VENTURE CAPITAL INVESTMENTS

VALUATION METHODOLOGIES

Valuation is defined as the process of identifying true value of an asset. Valuations are done in efficient markets so as to justify the price of an asset, whereas valuations are done in inefficient markets so as to understand whether the asset is fairly valued, undervalued or overvalued. Valuation also provides insights into the growth strategy of the companies as it helps in determining the appropriate amount of capital that should be invested in the form of capital expenditure as well as working capital. Valuation helps in budgeting and strategizing for the expenditure for M&A (inorganic growth), property plant and equipment, research and development and selling and general administrative expenses. This helps in understanding the re-investment amount and re-investment rate (discussed later in the chapter) in regard to year-over-year growth for the respective companies. Valuation further helps in strategizing the anticipation of the return on capital that companies intend to achieve for future years. With budgeting (by defining re-investment rate) and anticipated return on capital, the companies can determine the year-over-year operating income in years to come, which in turn helps in creating targets for sales, market, operations and finance teams of the companies. With joint efforts of the different teams in the companies, the management can achieve these targets year-over-year basis and

Figure 5.1 Valuation Methods

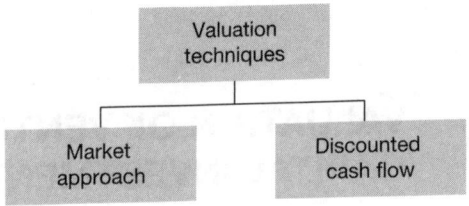

can actually increase the stock price of their respective companies on year-over-year basis. So, we can say that valuation is framework which gives immense clarity as to how companies can work in order to achieve stockholder value maximization. The VC investments are done in private unlisted companies and so these investments are highly illiquid in nature. Generally, these companies are sold or invested in as whole and not in parts, hence valuation of whole business at particular date will be highly insightful from the investor's point of view. Taking above mentioned criteria into account, we will discuss the two major valuation techniques that are used by venture capitalists. These techniques include market approach and discounted cash flow-based approach (Figure 5.1).

MARKET APPROACH

The market approach method uses multiples to determine the value of start-up business. The multiples used include enterprise value (EV) divided by revenue (EV/revenue), enterprise value divided by operating income or earnings before interest and taxes (EBIT; EV/EBIT), enterprise value divided by sum of operating income and depreciation and amortization or earnings before interest, tax, depreciation and amortization (EBITDA; EV/EBITDA) and marketing capitalization divided by net income (price-to-earnings [P/E] ratio). Many a time start-up companies go through many rounds of funding before these companies actually start generating revenue as well as profitability. The first and subsequent rounds of funding means that the companies receiving VC funding go either for series of rounds of funding from same investors or different investors before these companies become big enough to be either put on sale or go for IPO. The sale of business or IPO are two available options to venture capitalists as the medium of exit from their respective investments in companies. So, to understand the conceptual framework of valuation of start-ups, these start-ups will be valued from the first round and multiple rounds of financial perspective.

First-Round Valuation

In the first round of financing, the start-up is in initial phase of development with zero revenue. For the purpose of valuation of start-up itself, the profit and loss statements are to be built for the years equal to investment-holding period of venture capitalist. These profit and loss statements are projected cash flows which are anticipated to be realized in each year of investment-holding period of venture capitalist. The last year of investment-holding period is the exit point of venture capitalist and so it will help in determining the future value of start-up which in turn will help in determining the present value of start-up. The value of start-up in first round is calculated for both pre-money and post-money status. The pre-money valuation reflects the value of start-up before first round of VC funding and so pre-money value of start-up is value before it gets any investment funding into the business. The post-money valuation reflects the value of start-up post first round of VC funding and post-money valuation is done after every round of investment funding. The post-money valuation reflects the value of business after every round of investment funding.

For the purpose of building projected profit and loss statements for investment-holding years of a venture capitalist, a series of assumptions are made. These assumptions include investment-holding period of venture capitalist, total revenue attained in a particular year and operating margin, depreciation and amortization and net operating margin as a percentage of revenue. Once these assumptions are made the revenue, EBIT, EBITDA and net income are calculated for each of the investment-holding years as seen in Table 5.1.

The operating income, depreciation and amortization, net income and EBITDA are calculated using following formulae:

Operating income = Operating margin × Revenue   (5.1)

Depreciation and amortization (D&A) = D&A as a
percentage of revenue × Revenue   (5.2)

EBITDA = EBIT + D&A   (5.3)

Net income (NI) = Net operating margin × Revenue   (5.4)

As seen in the Table 5.1, the investment-holding period is assumed to be five years. So, revenue, EBIT, EBITDA and net income from the exit year, that is, the fifth year will be taken to determine valuation of start-up. Next step in valuation is to determine the multiple for each of the variants, namely revenue, EBIT, EBITDA and net income so as to determine valuation of start-up. It's the choice of venture capitalist to choose any of the variants mentioned above to perform the valuation. But for the start-ups that are yet to generate cash flows, the revenue as variant is preferred choice.

No matter which variant is used to determine the valuation of a start-up, the process and nature of determining the multiple for each of the variants remains the same. This means that multiples are determined in same manner irrespective of the chosen variant. The multiple is chosen by using bottoms-up approach in which we weed out a universe of four to five comparable companies that are affected by same economic conditions that are operating in same industry,

Table 5.1 Financial Projections

Investment holding period	5					
Year	0	1	2	3	4	5
Revenue		₹0	₹0	₹300,000	₹450,000	₹550,000
Operating margin		40%	40%	40%	40%	40%
EBIT		₹0	₹0	₹120,000	₹180,000	₹220,000
Depreciation and ammortization (D&A) as %age of revenue		5%	5%	5%	5%	5%
Depreciation and ammortization (D&A)		₹0	₹0	₹15,000	₹22,500	₹27,500
EBITDA (EBIT + D&A)		₹0	₹0	₹135,000	₹202,500	₹247,500
Net operating margin as %age of revenue		15%	15%	15%	15%	15%
Net income		₹0	₹0	₹45,000	₹67,500	₹82,500

in same geography and that are offering similar products and are in same revenue range.

Revenue Multiple Valuation

Let's work on determining the value of start-up by using each of the multiples including revenue, EBIT, EBITDA (also called unlevered multiple) and P/E ratio which is a levered multiple (see example of comparable companies' universe using bottoms-up approach in Table 5.2). The EV is called the value of business and by unlevered value multiples we mean those variables in the income statement that are not affected by the capital structure of the company. The variables that are not affected by the capital structure of the company are revenue, operating income and EBITDA. In this section, we will focus on EV/Revenue, EV/EBITDA multiple. So, to calculate the unlevered enterprise value multiple we will use the following equations:

$$\text{Revenue multiple } (R_m) = EV/Revenue \qquad (5.5)$$

$$\text{EBITDA multiple} = EV/EBITDA \qquad (5.6)$$

First, we perform start-up valuation by using revenue as a multiple. To determine the value of start-up, let's weed out a universe of five comparable companies which are affected by same economic

Table 5.2 Revenue Multiple Analysis

Companies	Enterprise Value (in ₹ million)	Revenue (in ₹ million)	EV/Revenue
C1	4.00	1.50	2.7
C2	5.00	1.80	2.8
C3	4.50	1.80	2.5
C4	6.00	2.00	3.0
C5	4.80	2.20	2.2
Avg. multiple			2.6

conditions that are operating in same industry, in same geography and that are offering similar products and are in same revenue range (see Table 5.2). As seen in Table 5.2, we have taken enterprise value as well as latest financial year's revenue and then divided EV with revenue to determine revenue multiple. Next, take average of multiples of all comparable companies and use this average revenue multiple to determine the value of start-up.

To perform start-up valuation using revenue multiple, let's take the revenue data of exit year from Table 5.1. In the Table 5.1, we can see that the investment-holding period is assumed to be five years and so exit date is also five years. This means that the venture capitalist plans to exit after five years from the initial date of investment. For the purpose of valuation, Table 5.3 is constructed by taking exit values from Table 5.1. The revenue multiple-based valuation is as follows:

Table 5.3 Assumptions

Assumptions	At Exit
Revenue at the end of investment holding year (exit)	₹550,000
Investment holding period	5
Revenue multiple (EV / Revenue)	2.6
Initial number of shares before venture capital investment	₹50,000

Start-up value at the end of the investment-holding period
(exit date) = Revenue × R_m = 550,000 × 2.6 = ₹1,430,000   (5.7)

Let's assume that entrepreneur wants to raise ₹60,000 from the venture capitalist at the initial year of start-up. The required rate of return as expected by the venture capitalist is 55 per cent:

Future value of investment done by venture capitalist at exit
date after five years = 60,000 × (1 + 0.55)^5 = ₹536,797

Considering the above investment in the initial year and the required rate of return by venture capitalist, we calculate the percentage of the start-up owned by the venture capitalist:

Percentage of start-up owned by the venture capitalist = Future value of investment done by venture capitalist/Value of start-up at exit = 536,797/1,430,000 = 38%   (5.8)

Now, let's calculate pre-money and post-money valuation of the start-up. Pre-money valuation is the present value of start-up before the net of investment done by the venture capitalist and post-money valuation is present value of start-up after the net of investment:

Pre-money valuation of start-up = Present value of the start-up − Amount of capital raised from venture capitalist   (5.9)

Present value of the start-up = Start-up value at the end of the investment-holding period/$(1 +$ Required rate of return by venture capitalist$)^{\text{Investment holding period}}$ (5.10)

Pre-money valuation of start-up = 1,430,000/$(1 + 0.55)^5$ − 60,000 = ₹99,837

Post-money valuation of start-up = Present value of start-up = 1,430,000/$(1 + 0.55)^5$ = ₹159,837

Post-money number of shares in start-up = Initial number of shares before VC investment/$(1 −$ Percentage of start-up owned by venture capitalist$)$ (5.11)

Post-money number of shares in start-up = 50,000/$(1 − 0.38)$ = ₹80,049

Share price of the start-up = Post-money valuation of start-up/Post-money number of shares in start-up = 159,837/80,049 = ₹2 per share.

EBITDA Multiple Valuation

The ratio of EV to EBITDA can be used to calculate the EBITDA multiple and check whether the EV is correctly priced in the market. This can be done by calculating the EBITDA multiple of the closest possible four to five competitors and then comparing the multiples with the multiple of the concerned company. The EBITDA multiple is a better measure for valuation as it is not affected by the changes in the capital structure of the company and so while comparing concerned company with its competitors, capital structure doesn't play any role. Let's say a company raises debt to buy back equity from the market and reduce the number of shares outstanding in the market, and if this happens then earnings per share will increase. In EBITDA multiple valuations, such a change in capital structure will not affect the valuation of the enterprise. Alternatively, if a company raises equity to pay off its debt then the number of shares outstanding will increase and so the earnings per share (earnings/total shares outstanding) will decrease which will eventually increase the price earnings ratio (price per share/earnings per share). In EBITDA multiple valuations such a change in capital structure will not affect the valuation of the business.

As seen in Table 5.4, we have taken enterprise value as well as the latest financial year's EBITDA and then divided EV with EBITDA

Table 5.4 EBITDA Multiple Analysis

Companies	Enterprise Value (in ₹ million)	EBITDA	EV/EBITDA
C1	8.00	1.50	5.3
C2	6.00	1.80	3.3
C3	7.40	1.60	4.6
C4	7.50	1.75	4.3
C5	6.00	1.85	3.2
Avg. multiple			4.2

to determine EBITDA multiple. Next, take average of multiples of all comparable companies and use this average EBITDA multiple to determine the value of start-up.

To perform start-up valuation using EBITDA multiple, let's take the EBITDA data of exit year from Table 5.1. In Table 5.1, we can see that the investment-holding period is assumed to be five years and so exit date is also five years. This means that the venture capitalist plans to exit after five years from the initial date of investment. For the purpose of valuation, Table 5.5 is constructed by taking exit values from Table 5.1. The EBITDA multiple-based valuation is as follows:

Table 5.5 Assumptions

Assumptions	At Exit
EBITDA at the end of investment holding year (exit)	₹247,500
Investment holding period	5
EBITDA multiple (EV / EBITDA)	4.2
Initial number of shares before venture capital investment	₹50,000

Start-up value at the end of the investment-holding period
(exit date) = EBITDA × Multiple = 247,500 × 4.2

= ₹1,039,500

(5.12)

Let's assume that entrepreneur wants to raise ₹55,000 from the venture capitalist at the initial year of start-up. The required rate of return as expected by the venture capitalist is 60 per cent:

Future value of investment done by venture capitalist
at exit date after five years = 55,000 × $(1 + 0.6)^5$ = ₹576,717

Considering the above investment in initial year and required rate of return by venture capitalist, we calculate the percentage of the start-up owned by the venture capitalist:

Percentage of start-up owned by venture capitalist =
Future value of investment done by venture capitalist/Value
of start-up at exit = 576,717/1,039,500 = 55%   (5.13)

Now, let's calculate pre-money and post-money valuation of the start-up. The pre-money valuation is the value of start-up before the net of investment done by the venture capitalist and post-money valuation is the present value of the start-up after the net of investment:

Pre-money valuation of start-up = Present value of
the start-up − Amount of capital raised from
venture capitalist   (5.14)

Present value of the start-up = Start-up value at the end
of the investment-holding period/(1 + Require rate of
return by venture capitalist) Investment-holding period   (5.15)

Pre-money valuation of start-up =
$1,039,500/(1 + 0.6)^5 − 55,000 = ₹44,134$

Post-money valuation of start-up = Present value of
start-up = $1,039,500/(1 + 0.6)^5 = ₹99,134$

Post-money number of shares in start-up = Initial number
of shares before VC investment/(1 − Percentage of start-up
owned by venture capitalist)   (5.16)

Post-money number of shares in start-up =
$50,000/(1 − 0.55) = ₹112,310$

Share price of the start-up = Post-money valuation of start-up/Post-money number of shares in start-up = 99,134/112,310 = ₹0.88 per share.

Price Earnings Multiple Valuation

The P/E ratio is calculated by dividing share price with earnings per share of the company (see Equation 5.17). As defined above, the ratio determines the multiple which can be used to observe the relationship of price and earnings of companies across the industry of the company by comparing the P/E ratios of the companies with each other:

P/E ratio = Price per share/Earnings per share. (5.17)

The P/E ratio helps in determining the multiple that indicates as to how many rupees an investor is willing to invest in a company so as to receive one-rupee worth earnings. This means that if the P/E ratio is 10 then the investor is willing to spend 10 rupees for 1-rupee worth earnings. While P/E ratio can be a great measure to evaluate an investment, it should not be the only measure to be used by the investor. A higher P/E ratio of a given company might sound like a great investment as the perception is that the company can earn higher profits in the future. At the same time, a high P/E ratio can be perceived as overvalued investment as promise of future returns might be over optimistic.

A careful analysis of various current and future projects and their viability to increase earnings to a level can be of additional advantage while choosing an investment. Also, higher the P/E ratio, more are the number of years it takes for an investment to return the price the investor paid to buy the share. So, with such perception an investor might choose to look at those stocks which have low P/E ratios. The low P/E ratio doesn't always mean that the stock is undervalued or as it will take lesser number of years for an investor to get back the price paid to buy the share.

The low P/E ratio can be because of bleak future or less promising future of earnings because of the nature of business and/or management of the company. Ideally, the investors can take an historical average data of P/E ratio multiple for companies in a given industry where the investor wants to invest and then create a data

Table 5.6 P/E Ratio Multiple

Companies	MVE (in ₹ million)	NI (in ₹ million)	MVE/NI
C1	6.2	0.25	25
C2	5.8	0.2	29
C3	6.4	0.25	26
C4	6.7	0.28	24
C5	6.75	0.22	31
Avg. multiple			27

set of highest, lowest, mean and medium value of P/E ratios of the companies in the particular industry. This can help in understanding the relationship of P/E in a given industry and help in making better informed decision:

P/E ratio multiple = MVE/NI $\hspace{3cm}$ (5.18)

As seen in Table 5.6, we have taken EV as well as latest financial year's net income and then divided market value of equity with net income to determine P/E ratio multiple. Next, we have taken average of multiples of all comparable companies and used this average P/E ratio multiple to determine the value of start-up.

To perform start-up valuation using P/E ratio multiple, let's take the net income data of exit year from Table 5.1. In Table 5.1, we can see that the investment-holding period is assumed to be five years and so exit date is also five years. This means that the venture capitalist plans to exit after five years from the initial date of investment. For the purpose of valuation, Table 5.7 is constructed by taking exit values from Table 5.1. The P/E ratio multiple-based valuation is as follows:

Table 5.7 Assumptions

Assumptions	At Exit
Net income at the end of investment holding year (exit)	₹82,500
Investment holding period	5
PE ratio multiple (market value of equity / net income)	27
Initial number of shares before venture capital investment	₹50,000

Start-up value at the end of the investment-holding period (exit date) = NI × P/E ratio multiple

$$= 82,500 \times 27 = ₹2,211,171 \qquad (5.19)$$

Let's assume that entrepreneur wants to raise ₹65,000 from the venture capitalist at the initial year of start-up. The required rate of return as expected by the venture capitalist is 70 per cent:

Future value of investment done by venture capitalist at exit date after five years = $65,000 \times (1 + 0.75)^5 = ₹1,066,851$

Considering the above investment in initial year and required rate of return by venture capitalist, we calculate the percentage of the start-up owned by the venture capitalist:

Percentage of start-up owned by venture capitalist = Future value of investment done by venture capitalist/Value of start-up at exit = $1,066,851/2,211,171 = 48\%$ $\qquad (5.20)$

Now, let's calculate pre-money and post-money valuation of the start-up. Pre-money valuation is value of start-up before the net of investment done by the venture capitalist and post-money valuation is the present value of the start-up after the net of investment:

Pre-money valuation of start-up = Present value of
the start-up – Amount of capital raised from
venture capitalist   (5.21)

Present value of the start-up = Start-up value at the end
of the investment-holding period/(1+ Required rate of
return by venture capitalist) Investment-holding period   (5.22)

Pre-money valuation of start-up = 2,211,171/
$(1 + 0.75)^5$ – 65,000 = ₹69,720

Post-money valuation of start-up = Present value of
start-up = $2,211,171/(1 + 0.75)^5$ = ₹134,720

Post-money number of shares in start-up = Initial number
of shares before VC investment/(1 – Percentage of
start-up owned by venture capitalist)   (5.23)

Post-money number of shares in start-up = 50,000/
(1 – 0.48) = ₹96,615

Share price of the start-up = Post-money valuation of start-up/
Post-money number of shares in start-up = 134,720/96,615 = ₹1.39
per share.

Multiple Rounds of Funding/Funding in Batches

Let's say a venture capitalist intends to invest in a start-up in batches
rather than investing lump sum amount at initial stage. Such
investments are done by observing the performance of a company
from one stage to another before next round of funding is given by
the venture capitalist. This behaviour of investing in multiple rounds
depends upon the progress of the company in terms of its goals set up
for each round of funding. But in such case, at each round of funding,
a new valuation is done as the previous investment has increased
or decreased the value of the business. So, this means that at each

stage of investment venture capitalist will get his share depending upon the current valuation, investment-holding period and expected return. Let's understand the multiple round funding with the help of an example (see Table 5.8).

Table 5.8 Assumptions

Assumptions	At Exit
Investment holding period, exit year	5
Net income at exit year	₹500,000
P/E ratio multiple	30

As seen in Table 5.8, the investment-holding period is five years, that is, the investor intends to exit after five years from the start-up. The net income projected at the end of exit year is ₹500,000 and P/E ratio multiple is 30.

$$\text{MVE at exit} = \text{Net income at exit} \times \text{P/E ratio}$$
$$\text{multiple} = 500,000 \times 30 = ₹15,000,000 \qquad (5.24)$$

Table 5.9 Structure of Each Investment Round

Investment Round	First	Second	Third
Year of investment	0	1	2
Required rate of return for each round of investment	35%	25%	15%
Amount of investment	₹500,000	₹700,000	₹1,200,000
Duration of investment	5	4	3

As seen in Table 5.9, the venture capitalist has structured his investment into three different rounds with first round of investment at the initial stage, the second round of investment at the end of first year, and the third round of investment at the end of second year. So, the initial investment will be invested for five years, the second set of investment is for four years and third set of investment is for three years (see Table 5.10). The amount of investment in round one is ₹500,000, in second round is ₹700,000, and in third round is ₹1,200,000. For first round required rate of return is 35 per cent, for second round required rate of return is 25 per cent and for third round is 15 per cent:

Start-up valuation at round of investment =
MVE at exit/(1 + Required rate of return at
particular round)$^{\text{Duration of investment}}$

(5.25)

Table 5.10 Shareholding Analysis

Investment Round	First	Second	Third
Start-up valuation at round of investment	₹3,345,203	₹6,144,000	₹9,862,743
Amount of investment	₹500,000	₹700,000	₹1,200,000
Share attained by venture capitalist at each round	14.9%	11.4%	12.2%

Start-up valuation at first round = $15,000,000/(1+ 0.35)^5$
= ₹3,345,203

Start-up valuation at second round = $15,000,000/(1 + 0.25)^4$
= ₹6,144,000

Start-up valuation at third round = $15,000,000/(1 + 0.15)^3$
= ₹9,862,743

Share attained by venture capitalist at each round
= Amount of investment at the respective round/Start-up valuation at the respective round

Share attained by venture capitalist at first round
= 500,000/3,345,203 = 14.9%

Share attained by venture capitalist at second round
= 700,000/6,144,000 = 11.4%

Share attained by venture capitalist at third round
= 1,200,000/9,862,743 = 12.2%

Total share of venture capitalist after third round
= 14.9 + 11.4 + 12.2 = 38.5%

DISCOUNTED CASH FLOW VALUATION

The discounted cash flow-based valuation helps in determining the value of business as well as value of equity by determining the present value of the free cash flows to the firm (FCFF). To determine the present value of the FCFF, we have to work on calculating two components including the future FCFF as well as the cost of capital (Weighted Average Cost of Capital [WACC]) which shall be used to discount the future FCFF (Figure 5.2).

Figure 5.2 Discounted Cash Flow-Based Valuation

Value of business	• Discounted cash flow-based valuation
Identify FCFF as well as WACC	• Future FCFF on year-on-year basis • Discount rate (WACC)
Discount-free cash flows	• Discounted FCFF so as to calculate the present value of FCFF for year-on-year basis. • Add the FCFF for all the future years so as to calculate the present value of business.

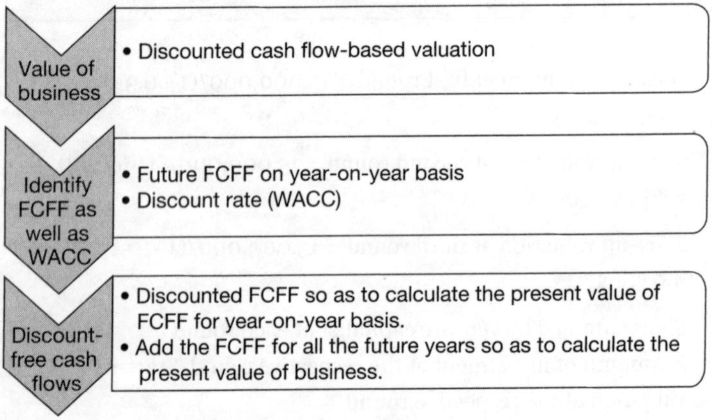

As discussed above, there are two components of discounted cash flow-based valuation. We will first work on determining the WACC.

Cost of Capital

The companies need capital in the form of cash so as to run their respective operations. This cash can be raised in the form of equity as well as debt. The equity is the amount of capital invested by the investors in the company and debt is the amount of capital provided as loan by financial institutions. So, there is cost associated with each kind of capital including debt and equity. The WACC is defined as the cost associated with the nature and amount of the capital raised by a given organization. By nature, we mean that whether the capital is raised in the form of equity and/or debt. The amount signifies the risk associated with the nature of the capital incurred.

The equity can further be classified as common equity and preferred equity. The common equity holders have the right to vote but their dividends are not assured whereas preferred shareholders have no right to vote but their dividends are assured. With three kinds of capital available in financial markets, the companies can raise capital in one or more of its kinds. The cost and amount of capital associated with each kind of the capital raised by the company combined together help in determining the WACC. So, we can say that the WACC is actually to the weighted average of all kinds of capital raised by the respective company (see Figure 5.3). So, we can write the WACC as described in Equation 5.26:

$$\text{WACC} = C_e \times W_e + C_d \times W_d \times (1 - \text{taxes}) + C_{pr} \times W_{pr} \qquad (5.26)$$

C_e: Cost of equity
W_e: Weight of common equity in the total capital
C_d: Cost of debt
W_d: Weight of debt in the total capital

C_{pr}: Cost of preferred shares capital

W_{pr}: Weight of preferred capital in the total capital

Total capital = Total debt + Total common equity + Total preferred equity

W_e: Total common equity/Total capital

W_d: Total debt/Total capital

W_{pr}: Total preferred equity/Total capital

Figure 5.3 WACC

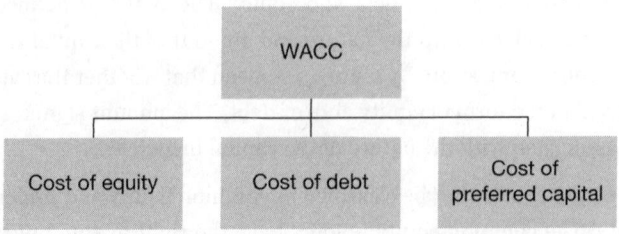

One by one we shall discuss the process of calculating the cost of each kind of capital. We will start by discussing the process of calculating the cost of equity.

Cost of Equity

The cost of equity is the cost associated with raising capital in the form of equity. In this section, we will discuss two methods of calculating cost of equity. These methods include bottoms-up approach and regression approach. First, we shall discuss the bottoms-up approach of calculating cost of equity and then after that we will discuss the regression approach of calculating cost of equity (Figure 5.4).

Bottoms-up Approach. In the bottoms-up approach, we work on creating a universe of five to six comparable companies which are trading in the same industry, offering similar products and are in the

Figure 5.4 Methods of Calculating Cost of Equity

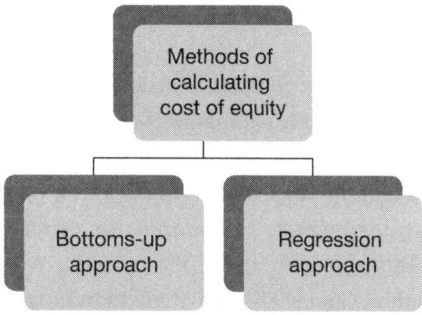

same revenue range (Figure 5.5). By same industry, we mean that if the concerned company for which valuation is to be performed is operating in banking industry then we should choose the universe of comparable companies in banking industry. If the concerned company is offering commercial banking products, then we should choose only those banks in comparable company universe that are offering commercial banking products and we should not take investment banks in comparable companies' universe. Moreover, from the above example of bank, we should take average of revenues for the last three years and then work on identifying the comparable

Figure 5.5 Bottoms-up Approach

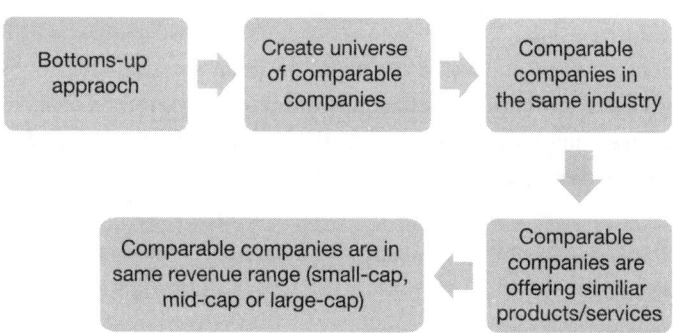

banks which are in the same revenue range. By same revenue range, we mean that whether the bank belongs to small-cap, mid-cap or large-cap.

Once we have created the comparable companies' universe by identifying the right comparable companies, we work on gathering information about β and debt to equity ratio of each of the comparable companies. The β of the stock defines the riskiness or volatility of the stock relative to the market. The information about β of any listed company can be taken from any of the following resources including Yahoo! Finance, Google Finance, Reuters India or Moneycontrol. The information about total equity and total debt of the comparable companies can be taken from their respective latest annual reports. After gathering information about β and debt to equity ratio of the comparable companies, we can use Equation 5.27 to calculate the unlevered β of each of the comparable companies:

$$\beta_{\text{Unlevered comparable company}} = (\beta_{\text{Levered comparable company}} / [1 - \text{Taxes}] \times \text{Debt/Equity}) \tag{5.27}$$

After calculating unlevered β for each of the comparable companies, we take average unlevered β of the each of the comparable companies (see Equation 5.28):

$$\beta_{\text{Unlevered average of comparable companies}} \sum\nolimits_{k=1}^{n} \beta \text{ Comparable company} \tag{5.28}$$

Then, we use β unlevered calculated in Equation 5.28 and impose the capital structure (debt to equity ratio) of the concerned company and use Equation 5.29 to calculate the bottoms-up approach β of the concerned company:

$$\beta_{\text{Concerned company}} = \beta_{\text{Unlevered average of comparable companies}} \times ([1 - \text{Taxes}] \times \text{Debt/Equity}) \tag{5.29}$$

Once we have calculated the β of the concerned company, we use capital asset pricing model (CAPM) to calculate the cost of equity of the concerned company (see Equation 5.30):

$$\text{Cost of equity, } C_e = R_f + (R_m - R_f) \times \beta \qquad (5.30)$$

R_f: Risk free rate of return
R_m: Return of the market

Regression Approach. This approach is followed in case the company is listed on the stock exchange. The monthly returns of the stock as well as monthly returns of the stock exchange can be calculated. The monthly returns of stock are taken as dependent variable and monthly returns of stock exchange are taken as independent variable, and regression is run to calculate the value of intercept as well as slope. The slope value is the value of regression beta.

Cost of Debt

The cost of debt is defined as the interest rate which the financial institutions charge for providing capital in the form of debt. So, the cost of debt can be defined as written in Equation 5.31.

$$\text{Cost of debt, } C_d = \text{Interest expense/Long-term debt} \qquad (5.31)$$

Another way to calculate cost of debt is to use interest coverage ratio. The interest coverage ratio is the ability of the company to pay off its interest expense from its operation income (EBIT). Interest coverage ratio
= EBIT/Interest expense $\qquad (5.32)$

Note: Generally, the start-ups are all equity firms with negligible debt and so cost of debt is zero.

Cost of Preferred Capital

Some companies raise cash in the form of preferred shares. The preferred shares are launched with a certain level of assurance to the investors that predetermined amount of dividends will be paid at predefined intervals of time. So, the cost of raising preferred capital can be calculated as seen in Equation 5.33:

Cost of preferred capital = Preferred dividends/
Total preferred capital (5.33)

FCFF Projection

For discounted cash flow-based valuation, we calculate the future year-on-year operation income (EBIT) so as to calculate the future FCFF. In discounted cash flow-based valuation, future FCFF analysis is done for two phases. The first phase is called the high-growth period and the second phase is called the terminal period. This is done for the very reason that no company can continue to grow at high-growth rate forever and therefore there is second phase called terminal period. To calculate the future year-over-year operating income, we have to first determine the growth rate at which operating income will grow in the future in high-growth period and so to calculate the future growth rate of operation income in high-growth period, we use Equation 5.34:

$g_{\text{Growth rate in EBIT (high growth period)}}$ = Future re-investment rate
× Future return on capital (5.34)

The future re-investment rate is the percentage amount of operating income minus taxes (EBIT × [1 − Taxes]) that will be invested back into the operations of the company on year-over-year basis for the high-growth period. The future return on capital is the anticipated return that company intends to generate on year-over-year basis over the high-growth period:

Future re-investment rate = (Future net capital expenditure + Change in non-cash working capital)/EBIT × (1 – Taxes) (5.35)

The future net capital expenditure is defined as the capital expenditure the company intends to do in the future in its asset base such as property, plant and equipment in the high-growth period. The change in non-cash working capital is the actual working capital requirement the company intends to have in the future in the high-growth period. The return on capital is defined as seen in Equation 5.36:

Return on capital = EBIT × (1 – Taxes)/Total Assets (5.36)

The companies can fix their re-investment rate and make a target of anticipated return on capital to project year-over-year operating income for the high-growth period (see Equation 5.37):

$$\text{EBIT}_n = \text{EBIT}_{(n-1)} \times (1 + g_{\text{Growth rate in EBIT (high growth period)}}) \qquad (5.37)$$

Once year-over-year operating income for high-growth period is calculated, the determination of future FCFF can be done by using following equation:

$$\text{FCFF}_n = \text{EBIT}_n - \text{EBIT}_n \times \text{Future re-investment rate} \qquad (5.38)$$

This way, we can calculate the FCFF for year-over-year basis for the high-growth period. Then, we can calculate the present value of the FCFF in the high-growth period by discounting each year's cash flow with WACC (for WACC, see Equation 5.26):

Present value of FCFF in high-growth period = $\sum_{n=1}^{n} \text{FCFF}_n/(1 + \text{WACC})^n$ (5.39)

As discussed above, the growth of company is divided into two phases including high-growth phase and terminal phase. In the terminal phase the company enters stable phase and starts to grow at economic growth rate, that is, gross domestic product (GDP) growth rate till infinity (it is an assumption in valuation that in stable phase the company grows till infinity and this assumption helps in identifying the equation for terminal phase valuation). So, for terminal period Equation 5.40 can be written as follows where the growth rate of operating income is known to us, that is, GDP growth rate:

$$g_{\text{GDP (terminal growth period)}} = \text{Future re-investment rate} \times \text{Future return on capital} \tag{5.40}$$

By using the anticipated return on capital for the stable phase the future-investment rate can be calculated for the terminal period. The anticipated return on capital can be industry average return on capital or market average return on capital for terminal period analysis as we can assume that in terminal phase the company will start to provide industry average return on capital. The future operation income for the first year in the terminal phase can be calculated as seen in following equation:

$$\text{EBIT}_{(n+1)} = \text{EBIT}_n \times (1 + g_{\text{GDP (terminal growth period)}}) \tag{5.41}$$

EBIT_n: Operating income at the end of the high-growth period
$\text{EBIT}_{(n+1)}$: Operating income for the end of first year in terminal period

The terminal value can be calculated by using the following equation:

$$\text{Terminal value (T.V.)} = \text{EBIT}_{(n+1)/}(\text{WACC} - g_{\text{GDP (terminal growth period)}}) \tag{5.42}$$

The present value of terminal value can be calculated as follows:

Present value of T. V. = T.V./(1 + WACC)^n (5.43)

n: Length of high-growth period

Using Equation 5.39 and Equation 5.43, we can add up the present value of FCFF in high-growth period and present value of terminal value to come up with value of business.

VC PORTFOLIO VALUATION

The venture capitalists invest capital in company with prefixed investment-holding period so as to generate return for their respective investors. During this investment-holding period, venture capitalists work with management teams of their respective investee companies so as to generate success in their respective ventures. This investment in companies by a venture capitalist is stated as portfolio of companies. The value of portfolio of companies is determined at exit by summing up the value of all investments in portfolio companies. The value of investment in a portfolio company is decided at exit time of venture capitalist and this exit value determines the rate of return generated from the investment in a respective company. Then exit multiple of a portfolio is determined by dividing amount returned to venture capitalist at exit by amount initially invested in portfolio company:

Exit multiple of investment in portfolio company (EM)
= Amount return at exit/Amount invested initially   (5.44)

The exit multiple helps in determining as to how many times the initial amount is generated as returned amount. This exit multiple decides the type of nature of success outcome from an investee company.

For example, if an investment in one investee company generated an exit multiple of 25 whereas another investee company generated an exit multiple of 5 then we can conclude that former investment is super success as it generated 25 times the return on amount invested whereas latter investment is normal success as it generated 5 times the return on amount invested. A venture capitalist can define the success of investee company in terms of the range of exit multiples (see Table 5.11).

Table 5.11 Exit Multiples Range

Type of Exit	Exit Multiple
Loss	$0 = EM$
Breakeven	$1 < EM < 5$
Normal success	$5 < EM < 10$
Grand success	$10 < EM < 20$
Super success	$20 < EM$

From Table 5.11, we can see that venture capitalist has defined exit multiple range to determine as to which category a return on an investee company belongs. Let's take a sample portfolio of companies of a venture capitalist to determine the overall performance of portfolio (see Table 5.12).

From Table 5.12, we can see the amount invested, amount returned, exit multiple and exit status of each of investee companies in portfolio of venture capitalist. Let's say that the venture capitalist raised ₹100 million for a period of five years and has five years to invest and exit from each of his investments. So, we can determine the value of portfolio after five years so as to conclude performance of the portfolio of venture capitalist. The venture capitalist invested fund amount worth ₹100 million and got a return worth ₹1,223.5 million, which is approximately 12.24 times the initial fund amount. With some

Table 5.12 Portfolio Analysis

| Company Name | Amount Invested | Investment Portfolio of Venture Capitalist | | Exit Multiple of Investment | Exit Status |
		Percentage of Portfolio	Amount Returned		
C1	₹8,000,000	8%	₹0	0	Loss
C2	₹12,500,000	13%	₹200,000,000	16	Grand success
C3	₹14,000,000	14%	₹0	0	Loss
C4	₹10,000,000	10%	₹75,000,000	8	Normal success
C5	₹10,500,000	11%	₹90,000,000	9	Normal success
C6	₹14,000,000	14%	₹0	0	Loss
C7	₹15,000,000	15%	₹850,000,000	57	Super success
C8	₹16,000,000	16%	₹8,500,000	1	Break even
Total	₹100,000,000	100%	₹1,223,500,000		

investments becoming zero at exit, some investments giving normal returns at exit and some investments giving exponential returns the overall portfolio of investments increased by 12.24 times at exit.

Table 5.13 Performance of VC Fund

Venture Capital Fund Analysis			
		Exit Status	Exit Multiple
Fund amount invested	₹100,000,000	Loss	0 = EM
Total fund amount at exit	₹1,223,500,000	Hurdle pass	1 < EM < 2
Fund multiplier	12.24	Normal success	2 < EM < 4
Fund status at exit	**Super success**	Grand success	4 < EM < 8
		Super success	8 < EM

The venture capitalist along with his financiers can define the success of portfolio just like venture capitalist has defined the success of each of investee company by looking at each investee company's exit multiple. As seen in Table 5.13, the financier along with venture capitalist have decided that fund will be considered as super successful if exit multiple of fund is greater than eight.

6

FUND STRUCTURE

On average, the lifespan of a VC fund would be 10 years. However, in some circumstances, it can be increased by a few years, depending on the situation where the funding for a business might still be underway. When opting for financing through VC, the entrepreneurs should understand that they will be provided with funding only for three–five years. Following that the venture capitalist would be more focused on providing guidance with regards to the management of the funds and only following up on the investments that have been made in various projects within the portfolio. This trend of investment has been around since the funding that took place throughout the 1980s in Silicon Valley. At that time, investors were mostly focused on investing in various technological trends existing.

The period for venture capitalists to raise capital for the funds from their LPs can vary from a month or two to several years. Once the investors and partners raise the required level of money that they would be using for funding various projects, the fund is closed, and following that point the lifespan of the fund is 10 years long. Many of these funds use the year at which the fund has been closed as a year of comparison when stratifying the funds in the VC.[1] The funds in VC can either be traditional, where each investor would be providing

1 Feld and Mendelson, *Venture Deals*.

Figure 6.1 Fund Functioning

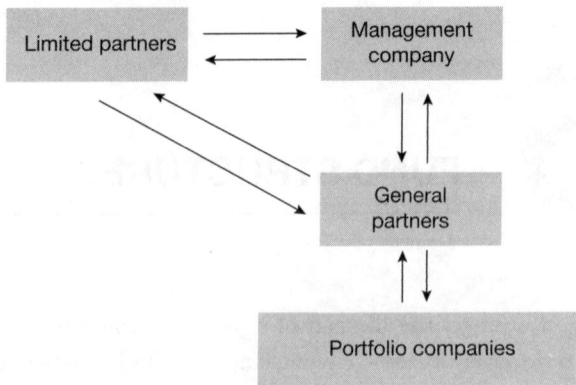

the same amount of money or asymmetric, where there are different terms and conditions for each investor. By and large, most of these funds have the same structure. Each of these funds is structured as a limited partnership, which is managed and governed by a partnership agreement among the involved parties. The partners are paid profit depending on the amount of their investment along with a carried interest. The structure of a VC fund includes the following parties and aspects (see Figure 6.1).

MANAGEMENT COMPANY

The firm that would be operating the VC is known as a management company. As the name specifies the company manages something, which in this case is financial resources and investments. This company is paid a service fee through the money in the fund.[2] This fee is used by the management company to pay the various expenses and overhead related to the operations of the firm. Some of the costs include salaries, rents, utilities and many other. The company can

2 Haislip, *Essentials of Venture Capital.*

make carried interest only after the LPs of the fund are paid their share of the investment.

Management companies can be seen as financial institutes, as they provide funds for investments and financial services. There are usually two parts of a management company. There is that part of the company which is responsible for raising and collecting funds from various investors, whether organizations or individuals. The other part of the organization is responsible for administering and investing these funds depending on the nature, expectations, and outreach of the fund. The two parts of the company are made up of entirely different individuals. The first part is composed of the investors of the fund, and the second part comprises various experts and managers responsible for managing and investing the funds.

The management company is an entity in itself, which works on handling as to how the capital collected is allocated across the variety of securities that are available in the financial market. The company is formed by individuals who have an understanding of financial services, funds and investment. These individuals include accountants, professionals in the venture, economists and various business specialists. These individuals fall into the second category of the business, as mentioned above. They are responsible for providing operational services and managerial advice to those responsible for the fund.

The company does not get any profit or revenue, unlike other companies. Rather, it charges a fee for the services that it provides to the fund and the investors. This fee is usually based on the overall amount of investment and funds managed by the company. These companies are managed and regulated by various acts and should be registered with the stock exchange of respective countries. The funds that the company generates should be registered to individual entrepreneurs, as well as corporates as well. These companies have a single offering as well as a diversified portfolio including various financial services, thus, enabling them to invest their capital in various projects.

A management company tends to have a positive reputation within the investment industry and the community. This can mostly be attributed to the fact that the company charges a minimal fee for its services within the market. Though some companies do charge a higher fee, it can be justified by their successful investments and the higher rate of return that they offer the investors through the varied investment portfolio. There can be different funds managed by the management company, some of which will be discussed here.

A management company offers investments to start-ups and businesses from a pool of funds raised. These shares of funds are purchased by investors, which results in a commission being charged for this sale, along with certain operational expenses as well. The funds managed by the management company should comply with the stock exchange and securities regulation authorities of the country. The regulatory body promotes fair activities within the market, educating the investors, and transparency at every level of the investment. The funds that such a company manages are either traded through the stock exchange, or through other management companies that are open-ended, which are commonly known as 'publicly traded investment'. These companies offer investors funds that are publicly traded in the form of a variety of standards and having investment strategies that are complex and beneficial. There are two types of management companies: open-end management companies and close-end management companies (Figure 6.2).

Open-End Management Companies

Some companies manage open-end funds known as open-end management companies. These funds are offered either as an exchange-traded fund or as a mutual fund. These funds do not have

Figure 6.2 Types of Management Companies

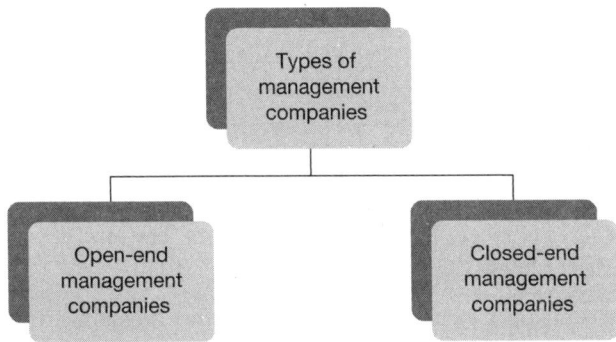

any designated number of shares that are available for trading. Instead, it is the company that decides the number of shares that can be issued and redeemed for an open-end fund in the form of an exchange-traded fund or mutual funds.

There are a variety of share classes that are being offered by open-end mutual funds. It is the responsibility of the management company to structure them with different types of fees that the investor would be liable to pay when making any transaction with an intermediary. These are not read through the stock exchange, and instead there is a company for these mutual funds that are responsible for the transaction of these shares. The transactions are presented and processed when the fund is being reported in the future at its net asset value; this is known as forward pricing.

As for exchange-traded funds, they are traded directly and daily through the stock exchange market. These shares and funds can be traded either at a premium or at a discount of their net asset value. There are also times when they are traded at par value. Authorized individuals of the company monitor the prices of these funds and the exchanges of the shares. These individuals have the authority to redeem and create shares at their will in order to manage the prices.

Closed-End Management Companies

Along with having open-ended funds, there are management companies that also control and manage closed-end funds. The difference is that these companies offer the market with a specific and predetermined number of shares through an IPO. These shares and funds also can be traded either at a premium or at a discount of their net asset value. In this sort of funds, managers do not create new shares to meet the needs of the investors. The market controls the price for these shares.

These companies focus on managing funds that are publicly traded. These funds can be managed through an array of varying strategies. The benefit of such management companies is that the funds are pooled, so are the management skills and capacities. Also, the company ensures efficiency through operation on the economy of scale. Unlike open-end management companies, these companies do not offer a variety of asset classes. These companies only have a fixed number of shares to offer to the market, which does not change. The company does not directly sell or purchase the shares. The fee structure of these companies is simple and straight forward in comparison.

LIMITED PARTNER

VC is comprised of various investors who come together to form a fund through which they can invest in various businesses. Those investors who can commit a certain amount of capital to the fund are known as LPs.[3] These partners are usually in the form of institutional investors, such as endowments, insurance companies, funds run by pensions, foundations, family-owned offices and individuals with a very high net worth. Although it is not the only partner in the fund, these partners do make an essential aspect of the fund.

3 Cremades, *The Art of Startup Fundraising.*

As the name specifies, LPs have a very partial say in how the operations of the funds will be carried out. Although these individuals and organizations provide all the funding for the management company, they do not have the right to make decisions regarding how the fund should be managed or controlled. As already mentioned above, LPs include institutional investors, individuals with a high net worth and family offices. The majority of the funds for the VC are raised through the pension funds. Each of the partners has the right to assess the funds before deciding whether to invest in it or not. The LP would be assessing the funds on different aspects. Some of these are discussed here.

The LPs of the fund would be interested in knowing about the asset allocation strategy that should be incorporated by the firm. This strategy would determine how the company would not be investing in the pool of funds that it has raised. The strategy would include several principles for the investment, along with guidelines regarding how the portfolio would be developed to help the company in determining the overall rate of return. VC is viewed as a category of private equity.

The investment criteria are another thing that the LPs would be determining. It includes the factors designed for assisting the LP in selecting the set of investments within every category of the asset. This can be the stage of the start-up at which the VC would be investing in, the sectors of the funds, or the geographical location of the funds. Understanding the criteria would help the investors in determining where and how to invest the funds that have been raised. Finally, the process of the investment is to be taken into consideration as well. This would include the timeline if the fund and the necessary steps that would be followed by these LPs to conclude with regards to the investment being made.

A LP aims to minimize the risk that is associated with the investment to a great extent and to target a substantial return on the investment. To ensure that the LPs on board have the capacity to do so, it is necessary to have the right mix of investors. It is the responsibility of the management company to ensure that the individuals selected to be LPs have the required decision-making skills. Identifying the right partners is the first step towards generating funds efficiently.

At times, the LPs in a new fund might only be individuals and family offices. Financial institutes are usually not interested in investing funds in a new management company, and this can be attributed to the difference in allocation strategies of the LPs. By developing an understanding of the allocation strategies, it would help with developing a useful framework. For instance, pension funds are the major contributor for VC, but they usually have individual reservations with regards to the allocation of the funds in the VC. On the other hand, foundations and endowments are more aggressive when it comes to allocating funds to the VC.

Any management company must understand that the competition for the fund is not only in the form of other management companies but it also comes in the form of various asset classes and the return based on the adjusted risk that is being offered to the LPs. The LPs of a fund have more impact and influence on the management company and its decisions than the cash that is available in the account. This is specifically true for the management company when it is in the initial stages of the business. There is usually the temptation for new managers to raise a large sum of funds, without realizing if the money being raised is right or not. The right set of LPs can have a significant impact on the fund and the capital that is being raised. It is the responsibility of the management company to ensure that the right individuals are being approached for this purpose.

GENERAL PARTNER

Apart from LPs, there are also general partners, who are direct partners of the management company. These partners are responsible for raising and managing a fund of the VC. Along with this, they also make the necessary decisions, determine the strategies to be followed, provide the firms they have invested in with necessary guidance and management and they also help them with exiting the fund. They are responsible for the latter as general partners have a fiduciary responsibility to the investors, who are the LPs. They are essential for the operations of the management company, as without their expertise and input, the fund would not be able to make the right investment decisions.

General partners are those individuals of the VC who own the fund to some extent as well as play a vital role in managing it as well. They are responsible for the day to day operations of the VC. Their role as managers of the fund and as advisors give them the authority to take the necessary decisions on behalf of the investors of the VC. At the time, it is not even necessary to let the LPs know of every decision that they make or take permission every time they have to make a decision on their behalf and for the operations of the fund.

As LPs have a limited say and liability towards the business and the decisions being made, the same cannot be said for general managers. Where they have an unlimited and free say in the decisions that are to be made for the benefit of the fund, they also tend to have unlimited liability for the decisions that they make for the fund. They are the first ones to be held responsible for the decisions that they have taken on behalf of the investors of the fund.

General partners are mostly professionals who have a thorough understanding of what to do and what would be expected from them as managers of VC. They need to have the necessary skills, abilities and knowledge to attract LPs, raise funds through them, and then invest them in projects that would ensure a high return for the investment that is being made. Though they have the freedom to make confident decisions on behalf of the LPs, there are specific terms and conditions that they would have to follow as well. It is not as if they can do anything and everything that they deem to be right.

They are responsible for the operations of the management company, along with investing a certain amount in the fund as well. They offer their services to the LPs and the start-ups for a predetermined share of the profits that would be generated through the operations of the business. Their share is very less than that one of the LPs, but in comparison to their investment, it is substantial, mostly because the return they get is not for their monetary investment, but rather for their efforts and skills that they extend to the start-up and the investors.

Their skill sets and knowledge is what makes them essential to the fund. They have very specialized information and knowledge about how to make a calculated investment that would be profitable, as well as guide the business towards success so that it could generate the returns that the partners anticipate. Along with their skills and abilities, these individuals also bring their pool of clients and contacts to the business as well. This helps the business in getting the required attention and support from various individuals and organizations.

Unlike LPs, general partners have many problems to face as well. For instance, if the business does not do well, not only would they be not paid for the services that they have extended to the start-up but they would also be liable to the LPs and for their investment. Thus, the investment decisions they make mustn't be based on guessing, but on proper calculations and strategic decisions. This is why the general partners are essential for the management company, as they have the necessary expertise and skills to manage the funds, invest them in companies with potential and to take the LPs into confidence.

These individuals are on the payroll of the management company. Along with the share of the profits, these individuals are also offered very modest salaries, which ensure that they make the right decisions and give their full attention to the VC. This can be justified on the basis that the general partners are paid the share of profit or management fee only when the organization can generate a certain amount of profits or returns for the LPs. Thus, they should be compensated for their time and efforts in making the investment a success.

TYPES OF FUNDS

The entire purpose of VC is to provide various businesses with investment to boost their operations and activities, at the same time providing them with guidance where necessary regarding the activities. VC can provide a business with funds depending on several factors. Though the stage at which a business is operating at the time of investment is a common determinant of the fund, which is not the only aspect of determining the type of fund. There are three types of funds that can be used for investing purposes under a VC source of funding (Figure 6.3). These funds are discussed in detail below.

Figure 6.3 Types of Funds

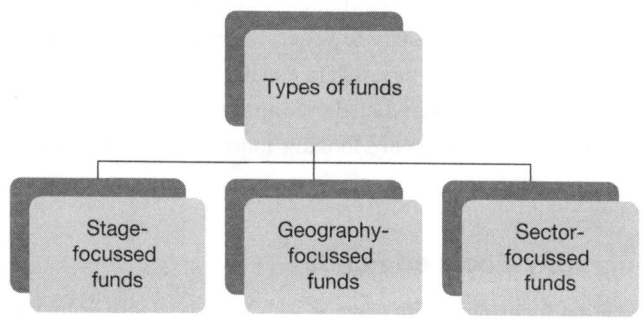

Stage-Focused Funds

The most common type of funds that a VC offers to the entrepreneurs and start-ups is based on their stages. These are funds that are given to start-ups depending on the stage of their life cycle. The most common stages are the early stage of a business, midlife of the business and the later or matured stage of the business. The funds that are offered to entrepreneurs who plan on starting up a new business is known as seed capital. These are funds that the VC keep for those ideas that are not yet launched in the market and would have the capacity to return huge gains to the investors.

Then there are those companies that have started their business and launched the product but require some financial assistance to continue the operations. These businesses are usually middle of their existence, but find it challenging to continue the business. Such businesses must have a very strong business idea and can execute effectively if they want to receive some assistance from the VC. It is not only the financial gain that such businesses would get but they are also provided with the necessary guidance and expertise of the general partners to make the right strategic decisions and help with the growth of the business.

Finally, VCs also fund businesses in the growth and expansion stage. VCs would only invest in businesses at this stage if they asses the business to have the capacity to generate significant returns for the business. Businesses at this level are usually well developed and have a clear understanding of what they want and how to achieve it. At this stage, the businesses are looking more for financial assistance than simple strategic guidance.

Geography-Focused Funds

Apart from focusing on the stage at which the business is operating, VCs also provide funds that are focused on a particular geographic location. The location depends on the nature of funding and the purpose of funding. For instance, funding businesses in a remote region, despite what sort of businesses they are, would be based on geography focused. This would benefit the VC by diversifying the portfolio and ensuring that the risk associated with the investments would be reduced. This is focused on the belief that the financial markets in different geographical regions might not be correlated with one another. This would ensure that even if the businesses in one part of the world are not doing so well, those in the other part will continue to grow and generate returns for the investors. This would help the company overcome the valleys and peaks in a particular geographic region, by diversifying the funds geographically.

The venture capitalists need to understand and evaluate the different geographic regions and determine where to invest the funds in. They should look at the things from a long-term perspective, rather than immediate and short-term perspective. This is necessary as the returns are not expected immediately, instead they would take a long time to materialize.

Sector-Focused Funds

Finally, there are VC funds that have been developed to invest in a particular sector of the economy or industry. Most venture capitalists are interested in investing in the following sectors: biotechnology, IT, medical technology, green technology and so on. These funds are usually structured as exchange-traded funds or mutual funds. These funds generally take the risk of investing in a sector with the hopes of it offering a high return to the investors. Specific sectors of the industry offer better potential for growth and as a result, better returns due to the investment being economically driven. This is an ideal way for VC to develop its portfolio companies.

Certain sectors would require the VC to have a higher level of due diligence as compared to others. Along with this, there are sectors within the market that do better when the economy is growing, thus investing in them is only beneficial at a time of economic growth. While other sectors are not affected by the conditions of the economy that much, such markets are stable. Although they might not generate a high return, it would be stable throughout the market cycles.

PORTFOLIO COMPANIES

The businesses or start-ups that VC has invested in through the funds raised by the LPs are known as portfolio companies. The funds that these companies receive are in exchange for a certain amount of preferred shares or equity. The fund will be able to get any return only in case of a liquidity event such as an IPO, an acquisition or a merger. These companies that the fund has invested in can be within the same industry or across a multitude of industries, depending on the nature of the fund.

There could be several reasons as to why a venture capitalist invests in a portfolio of companies. Mostly it is to gain profits, and at other times it is for depicting the strength that the fund has and the services that it offers to the start-ups and entrepreneurs. The portfolio of a fund can include both products and services being offered to customers in different markets and industries. The portfolio of a company is ideal for attracting new customers, creating a presence in the market and exhibiting how the business varies from its competitors within the market.

Businesses that a venture has exited from and that are successfully operating are a strong example of the success of the VC and its general partners. It is the responsibility of the general managers to ensure that the decisions that they make have a positive impact on the business, its profitability and success. Thus, if a business within the portfolio is successful, it would show the capabilities of the general managers at effectively and efficiently managing the funds.

Venture capitalists use portfolios as a business strategy that would depict the growth and development of the company, to attract shareholders and investors to the company. These companies can vary in size and form. From companies that need a boost in their capital to operate effectively to new start-ups that need the funds and guidance to set up the business and start running it, the portfolio consists of every sort of business. There have been many such businesses that have gotten the opportunity to make their idea a reality through VC. These companies cannot only develop new solutions to problems, but they also create jobs and give the economy a much-needed boost, with the help of the venture capitalists.

The primary purpose of investing in a portfolio is to ensure financial gains from a variety of businesses, rather than putting all the eggs in one basket. Although these businesses come with a high return, at the cost of high risk as well, however, a portfolio company that has the potential can offer the investors substantial returns of their investment. Once any of the businesses in the portfolio decides to go public or is sold off to another company, it pays off the investors with a return quite more significant than their investment. On average, the return that can be expected by the investor of a VC tends to be 30 times over their investment.

Investment Holding in Portfolio Company

Investment within a portfolio company can be made through various methods. The most common are discussed here, each of them being used for a different purpose and need. By having an understanding of these different methods for funding, it would be easier for the entrepreneur, as well as the management company to determine what sort of investment should be decided upon mutually.

1. *Investing through equity:* Venture capitalists look for such organizations and businesses to add to their portfolio who have the potential for growth and success and would ensure a level of diversity within the portfolio. Although investing in businesses that have started and are moving towards a growth spurt is a safer option, but at the same time, they do not offer the same level

of return as new ventures would. The general managers decide to determine which companies to invest in and at which stage to invest through equity. This is a decision which would have a significant impact on the pool of investment and the returns to the LPs.

2. *Buying a company:* Another way through which the investment can be made is through a buyout. Under such a decision, the VC buys a majority of the shares within the firm, and these shares usually amount to 51 per cent of the total shares. By doing so, the managing company gets control over the decisions of the firm. There are several reasons for a buyout, the most common being that the investors believe the assets of the firm are undervalued and reselling them would generate a profit. At other times, a buyout might take place because the general partners might feel like that the company could yield a high return, there is less competition in the market, or because the market is more comfortable to enter.

Steps Involved in Funding in Portfolio Company

There are different steps that the fund would have to go through before it can be finalized. The management company and the start-up would have to interact directly with one another to determine the deal and how to carry out the funding. The funding through VC is not something that would take a day for the general managers to determine whether they want to invest in the organization or not. Instead, it is a complete process of negotiations between the start-up and the management company to determine the terms for the funding, including the amount of investment, the rate of return, the exit strategy and role of different parties. The four primary stages of the process are discussed below to provide a complete understanding of how to get the required funding (Figure 6.4).

Figure 6.4 Steps Involved in Funding Portfolio Company

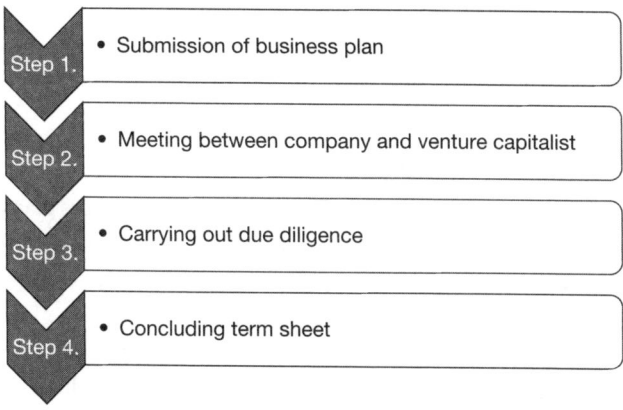

Step 1.
- Submission of business plan

Step 2.
- Meeting between company and venture capitalist

Step 3.
- Carrying out due diligence

Step 4.
- Concluding term sheet

Step I: Submission of Plan

The funding process of a business starts with the entrepreneur submitting a business plan to the VC firm. This plan includes all the necessary information that will let the venture capitalists know everything about the business, the idea behind it, the market it intends on entering, the product or services developed to be sold and plans regarding the growth of the business and profit making. In this stage of funding, the investee is responsible for providing any information that would make it easy for the investors to decide whether to invest in the business or not.

Most of the time, the venture capitalists would require an executive summary of the proposal, information regarding management, market size, financial forecasts and the competition and rivalry in the market. The process would move ahead only if the business plan has attracted the attention of the venture capitalists. Thus, while providing the necessary information, the investee has to ensure that it is presented in a manner that would attract and captivate the attention of the investors. Every aspect of the plan is essential; it should not have any irrelevant information, nor should it be unnecessarily lengthy as this would make it difficult for the investors to understand and stay interested in.

Step II: Meeting among Parties

Once the venture capitalists have been through the business plan and see a potential in the business idea only then would they schedule a meeting with the management of the business. This is an essential stage for the entrepreneur and the management to sell the idea to the venture capitalists and the management company. It is in this meeting that the venture capitalists would determine whether the start-up is worth the time and resources of the fund or not. Once the venture capitalists get all the necessary information and feel confident in the start-up and its ability to be successful and generate substantial returns, they would move towards carrying out due diligence.

Since it would be meeting in person, the business must present its case effectively and efficiently, while ensuring creativity. Venture capitalists are always on the lookout for something unique and exciting. This is something that the entrepreneurs should keep in mind when discussing the business, its benefits and the purpose of its existence. Investors would not invest their funds in a business that does not have a unique business proposition. The management of the business should understand this and provide information to the venture capitalists in such a manner that would captivate them.

Step III: Carrying out Due Diligence

Due diligence is an essential aspect of the deal. It is the audit or investigation about the potential business, its activities, partners, financial position, assets and any information that the business might have provided to the investors. It is the responsibility of the general partners in VC to carry out due diligence. In this stage, the venture capitalists evaluate all the information and references provided by the entrepreneur regarding the customers, the strategy that the business will incorporate, the creditors and debtors of the business and any other information that might have been exchanged.

This is something that the general partner should be comprehensive. It is their responsibility to access all the information that the business or entrepreneur has provided them with. Although the entrepreneurs and businesses would not mislead the investors, it is essential to cross-check and verify all the information being provided to the investors. If the information being provided is not accurate, those disclosing it can be charged with criminal activity and can be prosecuted according to the law of the country. Thus, this part of the deal, the fund structure and its evaluation should not be overlooked or carried out hurriedly. The general partners should take their time to assess the business and its capacity and to understand whether or not the investment would be able to offer the investor a high return of the funds.

Step IV: Concluding Term Sheet

Once the venture capitalists have evaluated the business, cross-checked all the information being provided and analysed relevant information, then they prepare an offering for the business known as a term sheet. A term sheet is a document that provides all the necessary information, including terms and conditions of the offer. It is a nonbinding deed among the involved parties. There is room for negotiation in a term sheet, and it is only finalized once both the parties are on the same page and agree to the terms and conditions that are being discussed by both.[4] All the necessary legal proceedings

4 Vries, Loon, and Mol, *Venture Capital Deal Terms.*

and documents are prepared once the agreement among the parties is finalized.

It is necessary to carry out due diligence of the business on legal grounds as well. As the venture capitalists should not be asking for information that is not relevant to the assessment of the business, nor should it overlook any information which would lead to incorrectly assessing the business. Following this, the VC can start releasing funds to the start-up. Thus, it is essential to discuss all the terms and conditions of the term sheet thoroughly, as once it is agreed upon, neither of the parties can go back on their agreements. This is the last and most essential stage of the funding for VC, and as a result, the general partners and LPs should both discuss the deal as well.

7

FUND ECONOMICS

V C is an essential source of financing for organizations. Although it requires time and patience, it is beneficial for companies in several ways. The venture capitalists do not only provide the start-ups with financial support, but they also provide them with necessary mentorship and help with managing the business effectively and efficiently. It is the responsibility of the general partners to ensure that the LPs benefit from the investments and that the management of the start-up does not make any decision which would have a negative impact on the investment. Thus, the start-up benefits from both the capital and expertise of the capitalists, making it relatively more comfortable to operate.

Without understanding the economics of VC, it would be challenging to understand its operations and activities. As already discussed, the VC is a very diverse source of funding and investment. To understand where the funds are raised, it is necessary to have a look into the primary funders of the management company. The VC would not be able to make it very far without its investors.[1] However, this is only one aspect to the economics of the fund.

To better understand how VCs work and how start-ups are provided with the necessary funding, it is necessary to have an understanding

1 Schell, *Private Equity Funds.*

of its economics. In this chapter, we will discuss from where the investors get the money, who are the parties that provide the necessary funds, why they do so, the returns that are generated, how they are generated and finally a look into the necessary rates at which VC fund operate.

PRIMARY FUNDERS

The funds provided to VCs are sourced by managers who have access to substantial pools of capital. These are the general partners of the management company. Although these venture capitalists do not provide a significant chunk of the investment, they do reach out to investors and motivate them to invest in the pool of funds. These individuals have the necessary resources, contacts and connections to reach out to various individuals and institutions that would have the necessary money to pledge to the fund.[2] Without the general partners of the VC, it would be almost impossible to raise a substantial amount of funds for the company to invest in its portfolio companies and diversify the investment.

The primary funders of the VC are its LPs. As already mentioned, they can be wealthy and successful individuals, or they can be various institutions who have capital that they can hope of getting a substantial return on it. There are many reasons as to why these investors contribute to the fund of VC. The primary reason is the substantial return that is associated with this sort of investment. Since these individuals pay for the majority of the investment in the VC, it is only fair to expect that the larger share of the profits generated through the business would be offered to the LPs.

The risk associated with new start-ups is usually very high in comparison to the risk associated with investments in public corporations and the period for holding is also longer. As a result, to

2 Green, *Venture Capital*.

make economic sense for the VCs, they would be expected to perform better than the public markets. As a result, the primary funders of VC are usually looking for a return rate that is at least from 5 to 15 per cent above the rate that is being offered to the public companies. To achieve this rate, the general partners play a substantial role in ensuring the businesses perform excellently and can generate the required revenue and profit.

Research shows that 80 per cent of the returns of a VC fund is generated by 20 per cent of the investments that the firms make. These 20 per cent of investments need to generate huge returns if it plans on covering up the lost cost of various projects that are either sold for an insignificant amount, or they are closed prematurely. To be able to earn more, there must be a high hurdle for each project and investment. This is something that the primary investors, as well as the management of a management company, are concerned about. No one investing their capital in a business and would want it to be lost, but at the same time, these businesses have a very high-risk rate. It is because of this associated risk that the investors expect a high rate of return, which usually does play out in their favour.

Without these individuals, the operations and activities of VC would not be possible as they provide the significant portion of the investment. Although the general partners also contribute the funds, it is not as substantial as that made by the LPs. This makes the LPs be the primary investors for the funds, also making them the receivers of the significant portion of the return that would be generated on the investment.

It is the responsibility of the management organization to evaluate the funders before they are approached and made part of the fund. It is necessary to assess their income and source of income, as it would help the investments. Along with this, it is necessary to make these individuals and organizations understand that if they are offering their capital, it would be for the long run as they cannot take it back once they have pledged it to the fund. Thus, these things should be communicated to the investors, who make up the LPs of the management company.

Without investment from these organizations and individuals who make up the primary funders, the management company would be unable to operate. Although they do not have a say in the operations and activities of the fund, their importance cannot be undermined. They are an essential component of VC, and without their financial resources funding, new businesses would become a challenging task. Many new organizations and ideas would not even exist if it were not for the LPs and their willingness to give funds to the VC.

HURDLE RATE

It is the minimum amount of return that needs to be realized before the profit of the organization can be distributed according to the conditions of the agreement. This is a rate which has been determined by the general and LPs when setting up VC. It works for the LPs in ensuring that the general partners would work to their maximum efforts to ensure that there would be a substantial return on the investment being made. The hurdle rate determines the minimum percentage of profit that the business would have to achieve.[3] For instance, if the hurdle rate is 15 per cent, it means that the business would have to make a profit of 15 per cent before the earnings can be shared.

The hurdle rate is determined because VC is mostly based on high-risk and high-return concept. Although the LP would be offered a higher rate of return than any investment that would have been made in a normal market, at the same time the investor would also

3 Kupor, *Secrets of Sand Hill Road*.

have to face higher risk as well.[4] As the risk associated with private investment is higher; thus, the investors tend to ask for a hurdle rate, before the fund managers can be paid any fee for their services.

When determining whether any particular project should be pursued or not, hurdle rate can play a vital role in helping the VC make this decision. It helps determine the suitable compensation for the risk that is being undertaken when investing in a particular project. Therefore, those projects that have a higher level of risk associated with them, the hurdle rate associated will also be high as compared to those projects that have a low level of risk. There are several factors that the general partner would have to take into consideration when determining the risk associated with a project.[5] Some of these factors include the following: the cost of the investment, the actual risk, potential returns for projects that are similar and any other factor that might have an impact on the investment being made.

For businesses, the hurdle rate is a significant aspect, specifically for new projects and future undertakings. Thus, the partners of VC must discuss this and come to terms with the rate that should be achieved in terms of profits. The risk that is associated with a capital project plays a significant role in determining whether it should be undertaken or not. For the investors and managers, if the project has a rate of return that is higher than the hurdle rate, it is considered to be a sound decision to invest in that project. Thus, they should determine and compare the two rates before making any decision. However, if the rate of return is less than the hurdle rate, it would not be a wise decision for the investor to go with the project, as it would be challenging for the investors to get a substantial return on its investments. Since the rate is trying to cover the risk with the return, it is also known as a break-even yield.

4 Gregoriou, *Encyclopedia of Alternative Investments*.
5 Bragg, *The New CFO Financial Leadership Manual*.

To determine whether a project is viable or not, the management company can evaluate it either through the net present value or through the internal rate of return. When using the net present value approach the cash flows of the business are discounted at a determined rate. This discount rate is dependent on the rate that has been used when discounting the future cash flow. The determined rate is the hurdle rate for the business. This rate is then used to subtract the total cost of the project from it, and the result is the net present value of the project being evaluated. The net present value that has been calculated is used to determine whether the project should be accepted or not. For projects with a positive net present value, they would be accepted as compared to those with a negative value.

The other method that is used for evaluating a project is the internal rate of return. The management would have to calculate the rate and then compare it with the hurdle rate that has been determined. If the internal rate of return is higher in the hurdle rate for a project, it will be accepted for funding. On the other hand, if the hurdle rate is higher than the rate of return for a project, it will be rejected for funding. Thus, when calculating the rate, care should be taken, as the future of the project depends on it.

Along with the above-mentioned methods, which are the most common ones used for evaluating the value of the project, another method is also used at times. When a project is solely financed using equity along with the present value, the net present value calculation of a business or a project based as a result is known as the adjusted present value. There are several benefits of using this method for evaluating the project, one of them being the tax benefit in the form of deductible interest. This is used to provide the investors with information about how they can benefit from the tax shields. Although this has many benefits, at times, projects financed through equity can have a less favourable outcome than those financed through debt when using the methods of evaluation. The adjusted net present value is the ideal method of evaluation when using leveraged buyout.

The hurdle rate is used to assess the risk and ensure a return for the risk being undertaken. To represent the amount of risk that the investors will be undertaking a risk premium allocated to the investment being made. The premium allocated for the risk can either have a positive or a negative value. The negative risk premium is used to counterbalance any factor that might be decreasing the attractiveness of the project, specifically if the risk associated with is not that less.

By using a hurdle rate to evaluate a project, if there is any bias towards a potential project, it can be eliminated. The investors can incorporate the hurdle rate in determining whether the project under consideration has any financial value and merit, irrespective of any intrinsic value being assigned to it. To achieve this, a suitable risk factor would be assigned to it. This makes hurdle rate a critical factor for investors.

CARRIED INTEREST

Also known as a performance fee, it is the amount of fee that is charged based on the overall profits that the business has earned. It is the share of the fund, from the net profit that the business has generated which would be remunerated to the general partners of the fund. This is seen as the management fee that the general partners are offered, which can range anywhere between 1 and 5 per cent. This is not the compensation that they are offered for the services that they provide to the fund, primary investors and the projects that are being funded.

Carried interest can be based on a single investment, or it can be based on the entire fund. The profits are split according to a ratio of 80:20. The 80 per cent is given to the investors, known as the

LPs,[6] whereas 20 per cent is paid to the fund managers, who are the general partners. However, the carried interest would be paid to the general partners only in case the profits generated through the investments exceed a predetermined hurdle rate. If this rate is not achieved, the general managers would not be entitled to the carried interest or performance fee.

For the general partners, working with a managing company, the carried interest is the primary source of income for them. On average, it can amount to anywhere from 20 per cent to 25 per cent of the yearly profit of the investment. Although there is a certain amount of fee charged for managing the fund, it is only meant for covering the costs that are associated with the management of the fund, excluding the compensation for the manager of the fund. Before the general partners can be offered the due share, it is their responsibility to ensure that the investment is returned to the LPs along with a predetermined rate of return.

To be compensated for the services that general managers extend towards the operations of the funds, they are offered a management fee, which on average aggregate to 2 per cent of the assets of the fund. The carried interest that would be paid to the general managers is a portion of their compensation that is paid to them after a certain amount of profit is earned.[7] This is an appropriate form of compensation for the general managers as they do put their time and efforts in all the companies within the portfolio by developing the businesses, guiding them to make the right strategic decision, and utilize the funds effectively and efficiently.

It is the general partners of the management company that is responsible for the various operational responsibilities of the start-up. The general partners would have to assist the start-up with developing strategies that would benefit the business, improve the

6 Stefanova, *Private Equity Accounting, Investor Reporting, and Beyond.*
7 Stowell, *An Introduction to Investment Banks, Hedge Funds, and Private Equity.*

performance of the management, make the operations efficient and maximize the worth of the organization keeping in view that it will be either sold or for its IPO.[8]

The carried interest that would be offered to the partners is not something that would be paid out automatically, and instead it is created only when the investment made generates several profits that would exceed the hurdle rate that has been determined among the partners. Unless and until the hurdle rate has been achieved, the general partners would not be paid the carried interest even though the LPs would be paid their share of the profits. Carried interest is termed as a capital gain for tax purposes. Therefore, it is taxed at a rate that is favourable for capital gains even though critics are advocating for the income to be taxed at reasonable rates.

The entire purpose of offering the general partners a share of the profits is to motivate them and give them incentives so that they would perform to their maximum capacity towards developing the business and improving its profitability. Even though these individuals would be compensated for their efforts; however, to ensure that they would not overlook their responsibilities towards the investors, these individuals are also offered a substantial portion of the profits. It is not as if these individuals would not make the efforts even if they were not offered this carried interest, but there would have been the possibility of them leaving for another management company or organization without this incentive.

ESCROW

An essential concept in VC is escrow. It is a legal, financial instrument that is used to describe the concept of a third party holding an asset on behalf of two additional parties. These two parties are connected because they have to complete a transaction that they are making.

8 Alworth and Arachi, *Taxation and the Financial Crisis*.

Under the terms, an agent would be required to hold on to the asset until the individual has been given any particular instructions, or any preset agreement has been fulfilled. The agent can hold on to a variety of assets, including money, funds, securities and other tangible assets. The duration and the reason for escrow can vary from project to project and investment to investment.

As already mentioned, the agent of escrow would be holding on to an asset until a transaction is completed between two parties. Since the parties are in between talks and transaction, there is uncertainty regarding who would get the ownership of the asset and whether the respective parties would be able to meet the prerequisite obligations or not, which is why it is handed over to a third party. The concept is used across the financial markets for varying reasons.

In VC, the LPs make use of escrow when investing their money. Rather than paying the VC directly the amount that they want to invest in a business venture, they can send them to an escrow agent and gave them instructions that the amount would be disbursed to the intended business, once the fund is closed and the start-up or business for investment has been selected. Instead of providing the general partners or the management company with the funds, the LPs send them to a third party, to ensure the security of the funds.

This is beneficial for the LPs in the sense that even though they might be the actual owners of the capital, once they pledge the amount to a management company, they have very little say in how to invest it and where to invest it. To ensure that the investment would be beneficial, the agent would disburse the funds only if specific prerequisites of the LPs are fulfilled.

The escrow provision in an agreement is also used in the circumstances where the funds might not do as well as the general partners might have anticipated. This provision is added to the agreement on the request of the LP. Along with being used to disburse the funds, the escrow provision can also be used to cover up the losses that the LPs might have to face in case the investment made does not do as well. Thus, it is a necessary provision that should be considered adding to the agreement that would be made between the partners.

CLAWBACK AGREEMENTS

While general partners are paid out a performance fee, LPs also at times demand to be paid in case any overpayments are returned in a situation where the investments do not perform well. These payments are in the form of clawback agreements. These provisions are added to the agreement between the general partners and LPs in case the funds do not do well. Such agreements justify it when general partners are paid carried interest as not being salary, instead being a return on their investment which is based on their level of performance.[9] Thus, if the LPs are being paid for the risk that they would have to go through, it only makes sense for the general partners to be paid as well.

Although performance fee or carried interest is easy to enforce when compared to clawback, it becomes difficult to enforce clawback when there is a significant financial hurdle, or they carry recipients that are not part of the firm any longer. Thus, this provision would have to be thoroughly examined and understood before it should be made part of the agreement between the partners. Having a provision which would become difficult due to any partner leaving or due to a change in the structure of the fund would make it difficult for the operations of the entire fund. Any provision that is added to the agreement should be thoroughly assessed and discussed from various perspectives.

The purpose of the economics of a VC fund is to make both the general partners and the LPs focus on future returns rather than focusing on existing cash compensation. This would motivate them

9 Sirkin and Cagney, *Executive Compensation.*

all to be concentrated on the gains and returns, which would help the entrepreneurs, LPs and general partners to align their goals, as they are all in the same boat. This is beneficial for VC funds of any size.[10] As the VC grows, the fees and numbers associated would increase as well.

This provision would ensure that the general partner develops strategies that would benefit the start-up so that it would generate profits to meet the set rates and percentages of profit. The general partners would not want that carried claw to be imposed, and so as a result, they will take a decision that will benefit the LPs and secure their investment. They will not invest anywhere and with high risk without a high return. This is one of the provisions that the general partners and LPs need to discuss and be specific about before they enter into any agreement concerning the fund.

The management company should be clear about the various rates, ratios and financial calculations that it would use when calculating the various aspects of the fund. By understanding these calculations as well as the expectations, the management company can hold the relationship of various parties efficiently and effectively. Neither there would be any unnecessary expectations, nor any disagreement with regards to what the partners be getting, the ratio of the profits and how they will be entitled to receive their shares respectively. All this makes it essential for the partners and the management company to thoroughly understand the deals.

EXIT ROUTE OF AN INVESTMENT

The venture capitalists plan exits even before investing in the particular business and that is how these venture capitalists are going to realize their profit in a given investment in the business. The VC would not be funding and guiding the start-up for its entire life cycle, and instead, it aims to get the business going and then

10 Arsalidou, *Rethinking Corporate Governance in Financial Institutions.*

eventually exit it. The VC would only be able to exit the business once the investment made can be cash pot fully. It would not make sense for the management company and general partners to exit a company while it has not realized its maximum potential and gains.[11]

The company and the partners have invested only so that it could generate profits. However, if this is something that has not been achieved, exiting would be futile, as it would waste the investment for the LPs.[12] Some of the methods that can be used to exit a business are IPO, M&A, selling the shares to new investors and buying back the equity (Figure 7.1).

The decision that the investors might make to exit the company would depend on several aspects. No matter the method that has been adopted, the final aim is to ensure a smooth transition of the ownership from the investors to the new owners. Thus, the strategy being incorporated ensures that the new and existing investors would not have to undergo undue stress and issues. It is a contingency plan for the LPs of the management company, as they would have to move to the portfolio companies once they have reached a predetermined condition.

Figure 7.1 Exit Routes of an Investment

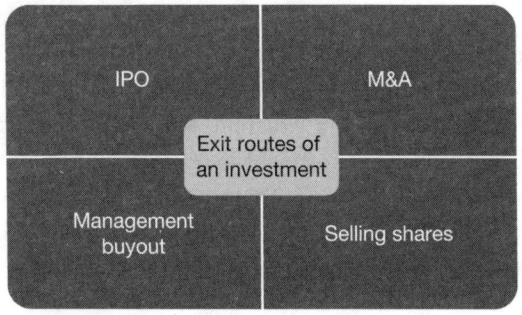

11 Demaria, *Introduction to Private Equity*.
12 Povaly, *Private Equity Exits*.

IPO

There are a number of benefits associated with the venture capitalists choosing to exit through an IPO. The major being that if the IPO is successful, it would be able to generate a tremendous amount of capital over a very short time, as the share value would increase. For new ventures, this is an ideal method to generate the necessary capital for growth and expansion of the operations.[13] With help from the general partners, the business would be able to go through an IPO at the right time.

Along with this, while the business would generate capital for growth and expansion, the LPs who have invested in it would also be able to receive their share of the return as well. These investors even have an option to sell their share of the business if they want to exit altogether. Also, by going public, the company would have the opportunity to attract more customers and work towards improving their brand awareness. Thus, the company would be able to benefit on different fronts when going for an IPO, while generating a return for the investors as well.

This is where several investors from the management company would want to exit the venture company, rather than wanting to continue with it. They would want to do so, as the value of their shares in the company might decrease with the initial offering, as a result decreasing their control and say in the organizational and strategic matters. In such a situation, they would instead exit the company and make an investment in another venture, rather than share their returns with others. This is an ideal exit strategy for such investors, as they would get their return as well as investment and leave the venture without having to deal with new management.

13 Khurshed, *Initial Public Offerings*.

Mergers and Acquisitions

The investors can exit the business when another organization decides to merge with it or acquire it. The business offering either the merger or the acquisition is quite often more significant in comparison to the business in which the VC has invested. Businesses usually merge to improve their customer base, operations and efficiency. It is beneficial for both the companies and their investors. For LPs, this is an ideal route to take when exiting a business venture that they have invested in. The benefit of this is that the business is usually valued at a high rate. This makes the business an ideal opportunity for competitors as well as other businesses to invest in.

For investors, this is a preferred method of existing as usually through this, they would be paid a substantial amount of return for the investment that would have made in the business when starting. There have been numerous M&A throughout history that depict the benefit of opting for this. M&A are mostly carried out within the same industry. This would not require the management employees of the business being acquired to go through a lot of operational changes, making it easier for them to adjust to the new business and the setup. For a successful M&A, it is necessary to have the management of the business on board with the decision being made, to ensure a smooth transition and overcome any hurdles and barriers through an effective manner.

One of the most common methods of exiting the company is through M&A. The company that would be willing to pay and buy the venture is usually a strategic company interested in buying businesses with potential. These buyers usually have a better understanding of how to evaluate a prospective company and whether the investment would be beneficial for them or not. Due to the potential of synergies and the strategic fit that these buyers have, they at times can offer a premium for the companies as well.

Selling Shares

Once the company goes public and if the investor has not sold their share of the organization as of yet they can do that at any point to exit from the business. The LPs can sell their share of the business to new investors completely separating themselves from the business and its operations. Although the investors can do this at the time of IPO as well if due to any reason they could not, they always have the option for selling of their shares to other investors at any time.

The shares can also be sold to existing shareholders of the company, increasing their ownership of the business. This is beneficial for investors as well as the existing shareholders. The investors would be able to generate more income for themselves by selling off the shares, and they would know that the individuals they are selling the shares to would make decisions that would be beneficial for the business that they had invested in. The decision to sell the shares to existing or new shareholders is a decision that the LPs will make on their own. The purpose of selling is, for the investors, to exit the company following the completion of their objective of earning a return on their investment.

This strategy of exit is also known as a secondary sale, as the management and confident investors might continue to hold on to their shares. This shows that it is not mandatory for all the investors of the company to sell their shares in the business, preferably even a single investor can opt for this route. It might not have the capacity of a trade sale, and the opportunities it has for synergies, but it could be an ideal option for the investors if they no longer want to be associated with any business.

Management Buyout

This is another method through which the investors can exit the business. In this, it is the existing managers of the business who buy the shares from the investors. The management decides to buy the business as there is a better opportunity for reward, and they would have better control over the decisions being made if they become owners of the business rather than mere employees. This is a favourable exit strategy for investors who will not retire from the business. The management can raise the capital for the buyout either through other investors or the new buyers.

In a management buyout, it is the internal management of the organization that makes the buying decision and buys the shares of the company, rather than having external management come and buy the shares of the business. The benefit that this would have for the organization is that the managers would not have to learn about the organization or to learn to manage it effectively. Since the managers would have an invested interest in the company, they would work towards developing strategies that would benefit the organization in the long run.

Most of the time, management buyout is financed by private equities who see the potential in the organization and decide to capitalize on it by encouraging it to go private. Once the business goes private and reaches the capacity, it would create the opportunity to initiate a public offering through which the shares would be sold, and capital would be generated.

The exit strategy that the management company decides will depend on the limited and general partners. They must examine the exit strategy thoroughly so that the investors would be provided with a return on the investment that they had made. The strategy that the management company decides to use when exiting a business also depends on the nature of the business and the industry to a certain extent. The same strategy cannot be used by investors to exit from every sort of a business, and this might result in a loss for the business and the investors. The time and the conditions of the market should also be taken into consideration when exiting business to ensure everything plays out for the business.

FUND ECONOMICS: PAYOUT MODEL

In this last part of the chapter, we will discuss as to how the payouts are structured in fund economics of VC fund. To understand fund economics practically let us take an example of a fund named ABC Inc. The ABC Inc. has four general partners who have worked along with the management company to raise VC for its fund (see Table 7.1). The general partners raised capital from four independent LPs (see Table 7.1).

As seen in Table 7.1, the total amount of capital raised in venture fund is ₹24.6 million. Out of total fund amount of ₹24.6 million, the LPs have invested ₹21 million and rest of ₹3.6 million is invested by general partners (see Table 7.2). The percentage share of each of general partners and LPs can be seen in Table 7.2.

The annual management fees charged by the general partners and the management company is 2 per cent of the fund amount. The

Table 7.1 Fund Investment Analysis

Type of Investor	Amount Invested in Fund
LP 1	₹4,000,000
LP 2	₹6,000,000
LP 3	₹6,000,000
LP 4	₹5,000,000
GP 1	₹800,000
GP 2	₹800,000
GP 3	₹1,000,000
GP 4	₹1,000,000
Total fund amount	**₹24,600,000**

Table 7.2 Fund Analysis

Annual Management Fees	2%	
	Fund Analysis	
Limited Partners (LP) Analysis		**General Partners (GP) Analysis**
Total fund amount invested by LPs	₹21,000,000	Total fund amount invested by GPs	₹3,600,000
%age of fund invested by LP 1	16%	%age of fund invested by GP 1	3%
%age of fund invested by LP 2	24%	%age of fund invested by GP 2	3%
%age of fund invested by LP 3	24%	%age of fund invested by GP 3	4%
%age of Fund Invested by LP 4	20%	%age of fund invested by GP 4	4%
Total %age of fund invested by LPs	85%	Total %age of fund invested by GPs	15%
Total fees charged over life of fund	₹4,920,000	**Total amount invested net of fees**	₹19,680,000

total yearly maintenance fees charged amounts to ₹492,000 and total amount charged as maintenance fees over the life of the fund is ₹4,920,000 (see Table 7.3).

As part of fund economics depending upon percentage of management fees fixed at time of inception of the fund, each of the general partners and the management company are giving fund maintenance expenses accordingly. The percentage of fee paid to each of the general partners and management over the life of fund can be seen in Table 7.4.

Last part of fund economics is to analyse profit shared by each of the parties involved in the fund. At the end of life of fund, total amount generated by exiting all the investments are calculated so as to determine distributed to paid-in capital ratio. The distributed to paid-in capital ratio is total fund amount given to particular investors at exit divided by total investment in the fund:

Total amount invested in the fund = Fund amount
– Management fees = 24,600,000 – 4,920,000
= ₹19,680,000   (7.1)

Distributed to paid-in capital ratio
= Total amount of fund given to investor at
exit/Total amount invested in the fund   (7.2)

At exit, the total fund amount was ₹236,160,000 and so distributed to paid-in capital ratio comes out to be 12 (Table 7.5).

Distributed to paid-in capital ratio of fund
= 236,160,000/19,680,000 = 12

The carried interest of each of general partners and management company are fixed at fund inception and same can be seen in Table 7.5. Based on carried interest of each of the general partners and

Table 7.3 Management Fees Analysis

Year	1	2	3	4	5	6	7	8	9	10
Amount of fees charged annually	₹492,000	₹492,000	₹492,000	₹492,000	₹492,000	₹492,000	₹492,000	₹492,000	₹492,000	₹492,000
Total fees charged over life of fund	₹4,920,000									

Table 7.4 Fees Analysis for General Partners and Management Company

Type of Manager	Total %age of Fee Paid over Life of Fund	Amount of Fees Paid over Life of Fund
GP 1	15%	₹738,000
GP 2	15%	₹738,000
GP 3	20%	₹984,000
GP 4	20%	₹984,000
Management company	30%	₹1,476,000
Total	100%	₹4,920,000

management company, we calculate the profit payout for each of the general partners and management (see Table 7.5). Also, we club profit payout with fees payout (see Table 7.4) for each of general partners and management company to calculate the total amount paid to general partners and management company from inception to close of venture fund (see Table 7.5). Next, we calculate the total amount returned to LPs so as to determine the distribution to paid-in capital ratio for all LPs.

Total amount returned to LPs = Total fund amount at exit − Carried payout = ₹182,040,000

Management fees paid from LPs capital
= Total management fees × Percentage share of LPs
= 4,920,000 × 0.85 = ₹4,200,000

Total amount invested by LPs = 21,000,000 − 4,200,000
= ₹16,800,000

Distributed to paid-in in capital for LPs
= 182,040,100/16,800,000 = 10.84

Table 7.5 Performance-Based Payout Analysis

Performance-Based Payout Analysis				
Distributed to paid in capital ratio	12			
Total fund amount at maturity	₹295,200,000			
Carried interest	20%			
Carried payout	₹54,120,000			
	Carried Interest	**Carried Payout**	**Fees Payout**	**Total Payout**
Payment to GP 1	20%	₹10,824,000	₹738,000	₹11,562,000
Payment to GP 2	20%	₹10,824,000	₹738,000	₹11,562,000
Payment to GP 3	25%	₹13,530,000	₹984,000	₹14,514,000
Payment to GP 4	25%	₹13,530,000	₹984,000	₹14,514,000
Management company	10%	₹5,412,000	₹1,476,000	₹6,888,000
Total	100%	₹54,120,000	₹4,920,000	₹59,040,000

Finally, we calculate the multiple of total capital actually invested and net of management fees and this multiple reflects as to how many times the capital invested has multiplied.

Multiple of capital invested = Fund amount at inception × Distributed paid-in capital ratio/Total amount of capital invested in the fund
= 24,600,000 × 12/19,680,000 = 15

8

HOW VENTURE CAPITAL FUNDS RAISE CAPITAL

A s stated in the earlier chapters, the VC funds raise capital from partners which include institutional investors such as endowments, insurance companies, funds run by pensions, foundations, family-owned offices and individuals with a very high net worth. These LPs study various aspects of VC fund before they decide providing venture capitalists with capital. The reason to study various aspects is to understand as to whether investment goals and investment style of LP matches with that of general partners' fund.

The investment goals and investment styles of LPs vary and so prospectus helps in determining whether a particular fund is appropriate for LPs investment needs. The investment goals and investment styles of limited partner vary as they intend to invest in venture funds with differentiating risk profiles. The differentiating risk profiles mean that some LPs are comfortable investing in seed capital fund whereas other LPs are more comfortable investing in little mature and established start-ups in terms of product development. The investment goals of LPs also include particular kind of companies or industries that they would like to include in their investment portfolio. These various aspects are put together in the form of the prospectus by the venture capitalist.

This prospectus provides all the relevant information regarding the VC firm and its owners that's necessary for LPs to know before they decide funding the VC firm. The venture capitalists establish contact with LPs and take appointments to give presentations and provide prospectuses of their funds so as to raise capital. The prospectus, in particular, helps LPs in understanding the team of VC firm (general partners) as well as fund intricacies and details even before the venture capitalists are allowed to give a presentation to LPs. Also, the prospectus is direct marketing material for funds which is supplied to LPs so that they can have an understanding of the historical performance of the fund as well. The decision-making process of LPs involves two major factors including general partner's team, fund intricacies and details (see Figure 8.1).

The prospectus should be written in such a manner as if through the prospectus, the general partners are answering all the questions which will arise as part of due diligence and decision-making process of LP. This way prospectus helps immensely in the fund-raising process and saves time for both limited as well as general partners. In the next part of the chapter, we will discuss prospectus from the assessment of general partners. This assessment also reflects as to what content should be present in the prospectus so that all the information is given to LPs transparently.

Figure 8.1 Fund Prospectus for VC Fund Raising

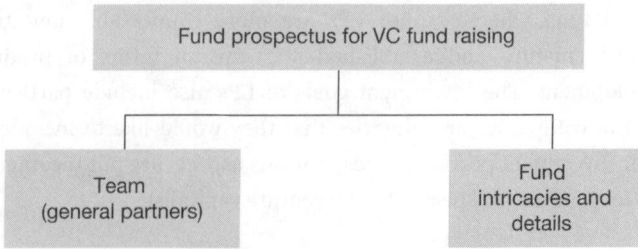

GENERAL PARTNERS' TEAM

As part of general partner's team, the prospectus should cover past performance, experience, venture development know-how, market network and market reputation of general partners. The first and foremost question that arises in the assessment of general partners is the track record of past performances in previous funds. So, the prospectus should mention all the details of each of the VC funds previously managed by the respective general partners. The past performance of the general partner is assessed in terms of not only the overall performance of previous funds but also by assessing the performance of each of the investee companies in each of the previous funds. This assessment is done so as to understand as to how many investments in a particular fund were successful and how many were a failure. This assessment of the performance of each company in particular fund is done so as to understand whether a fund performed well because of the overall performance of investee companies or because of one boom investment return from just one particular investee company.

For example, in a historical performance analysis of a particular fund of general partners shows that investment was done in 10 companies over the life of the fund and analysed that it gave a return of 30 times the total initial investment. However, when dig down on each of the investee company is done then it is realized that out of 10 companies 8 were failures, 1 gave a return of just 5 times and 1 investment was super boom with a return of 300 times. In such cases, it can be said that overall the general partners were unable to identify good investee companies as 8 out of 10 failed to deliver even the total initial investment and so only performance of 1 company is showing that fund was a success. Such a success coming from only 1 investee company out of a total of 10 is not considered as a successful fund by LPs as 8 investments failed and just 1 investment gave enough return to make fund successful. Let us take another example of a historical performance analysis of one of the funds of a particular general partner. The analysis showed that fund invested in 8 companies over the life of fund and out of these 8 investments 4 became redundant and 4 gave a success of 12 times the initial capital invested. This particular fund is considered more successful as general partners were able to find such investee companies where 50 per cent of them were successful though they gave a return of 12 times which is less than pervious fund manager's return of 30 times. This is because the fund manager who gave 30 times return created most of the return from a single investment and 8 per cent of his/her investment became redundant.

Also, many a time general partners who intend to raise capital for the next fund had run more than one fund. In such cases, LPs analyse each of the performance of each previous funds from overall as well as investee companies' point of view. The LP will analyse the performance of each of the fund and relate to a number of successful investments in each of the funds. This will give clarity as to how many investments in each of the funds are successful. Such information helps LPs in determining the ability of the general partner to identify profitable investee companies. Let us take an example of two general partners including ABC Inc. and XYZ Inc. so as to understand better analysis of general partners who ran more than one fund historically (see Tables 8.1 and 8.2). Case I shows that this particular general partner had run five funds historically and the failure rate ranges from 50 to 60 per cent whereas for case II shows that this particular general partner had also run five funds historically and the failure rate ranges from 70 to 80 per cent. So, the crux of their ability to identify right investee companies shows that general partners at ABC Inc. are better off than their counterparts at XYZ Inc. Although each of the funds of XYZ Inc. has given more return than each of the funds of ABC Inc., the former is a more risky investor, and it gets luck to have one or two boom returns so

Table 8.1 CASE I: Performance Analysis of Funds of ABC Inc.

Case I: General Partners (ABC Inc.)						
Fund	Amount Invested	Return Times	Total Invesments	Successes Analysis		
				Normal Success	Super Boom	Failure
Fund I	₹100,000,000	12	10	3	2	5
Fund II	₹200,000,000	25	10	2	2	6
Fund III	₹400,000,000	14	10	3	1	6
Fund IV	₹300,000,000	15	10	4	1	5
Fund V	₹350,000,000	16	10	5	0	5

Table 8.2 CASE II: Performance Analysis of Funds of XYZ Inc.

Case II: General Partners (XYZ Inc.)						
Fund	Amount Invested	Return Times	Total Invesments	Successes Analysis		
				Normal Success	Super Boom	Failure
Fund I	₹100,000,000	15	10	0	2	8
Fund II	₹200,000,000	30	10	1	2	7
Fund III	₹400,000,000	16	10	2	1	7
Fund IV	₹300,000,000	18	10	2	1	7
Fund V	₹350,000,000	22	10	1	2	7

that overall performance of the fund is higher. The prospectus of general partners needs only to mention performance of each of the respective funds and need not mention about the performance of their competitors, but LPs do perform such analysis before providing funds to general partners.

Next, the prospectus should mention all the details regarding the choice of investments they make. This choice mentions a particular kind of industries that are targeted for investment purpose. This choice also includes the stage of investee companies in which general partners invest. By stage, it means that whether general partners prefer investee companies that need angel, pre-seed, seed, series unknown, series A or B or series C funding. Also, as a part of investment objectives and style, the VC fund should declare its benchmark. This benchmark's returns are compared with the fund's returns to determine the performance of the respective fund.

The prospectus also mentions the role of general partners in the management of each of investee companies. This part of the prospectus enlightens the LPs about the fact that how many general partners and management team members are part of the VC fund and out of these, how each of them is working with investee companies. For example, a VC fund is planning to raise more capital for another fund, but each of the general partners is already on board with three companies. Such information is always required as LPs want to know about the availability of general partners for the fund they plan to invest in.

As part of the team of general partners, the prospectus should include the resumes of each of the general partners. These resumes should be written extensively mentioning in detail and in-depth knowledge and experience of each of the general partners involved in the VC fund. The past experience of general partners should not only mention their ability to successfully run start-ups but also their ability to understand industry dynamics of several start-ups.

The resumes should reflect as to how many start-up/immature companies that each of them has run in the past and if there were any boom returns with star performance, then every one of such boom-return investee companies should be mentioned. Such in-depth detailed resumes help LPs understand as to whether the general partners are experienced enough in terms of their respective knowledge about start-ups/immature companies and industries in which they intend to invest.

Many a time more than two VC funds invest in a single start-up to take benefit of each other's experience and knowledge and to reduce the risk of losing the amount of capital invested. Such an arrangement is possible only if the venture capitalists of two different funds are not only comfortable with each other but also share great repo and respect for each other. Also, a venture capitalist who invested in a particular stage of investee company likes to exit when a company reaches a particular stage. Many a time in such cases the venture capitalists sell their respective share to later stage venture capitalists. For example, a pre-see venture capitalist plans to exit an investee company when it researches series C round of funding and so would like to sell his share to a later stage venture capitalist. So, for such scenarios mentioned above market networking is very important where other venture capitalists are not only comfortable working on joint investment but only are willing to buy respective investments.

The venture capitalists with excellent reputation in the market are seen as safe investments not only by investors but also are perceived as good partners by investee companies/entrepreneurs. The venture capitalists that follow good practices in valuations (information asymmetry in Chapter 1) are considered as honest partners as they will not cheat in percentage share allotment with entrepreneurs at times of entry as well as exit. The venture capitalists that follow malpractice in valuations will eventually bring bad names for themselves, and they will generate a bad reputation and perception for themselves in the market. The venture capitalists who are well connected in the market and who help entrepreneurs in the better running of their companies bring good names for themselves in the market and so such reputation will attract good entrepreneurs/investee companies in the future. So, to better market themselves, the venture capitalist should run free campaigns, valuation awareness seminars and events to create awareness about their fund among entrepreneurs. Such campaigns, seminars and events should be mentioned in the prospectus as it will be considered as a positive step by LPs.

FUND INTRICACIES AND DETAILS

In this part of the chapter, we will discuss the second part of the prospectus which includes fund intricacies and details. The fund intricacies and details will cover management fees, carried interest, capital in the fund, the proportion of the contribution of general partners in fund, number of portfolio companies targeted, the proportion of capital invested in each of the portfolio companies, investment style and deal evaluation process.

In this prospectus, the VC firm should mention management fees charged for each of the previous funds that they have managed. Also, the prospectus should include the management fees that will be charged for the next fund that venture capitalists are planning to raise. The bifurcation of management fees should be clearly stated. The bifurcation of management fees should include the percentage of total fees to be paid to each of the general partners as well as the management company (fund economics Chapter 7). Many a time, management fees as a percentage of the fund amount (let's say for example 2% of the fund amount) does not remain same over the life of the fund. So, if the life of the fund is 10 years, the management fee for the first five years is sometimes different from the next five years. If that is the case, then it should be mentioned as to how much would be management fees for what part of the life of the fund.

In this prospectus, the VC firm also should mention carried interest charged for each of the previous funds that they have managed. This carried interest should be mentioned not only in terms of percentage of profit but also in terms of total profit amount taken by the general partners in each of the previous funds. Also, the prospectus should include the carried interest that will be charged for the next fund that venture capitalists are planning to raise, and this carried interest should be compared to industry norms of venture capitalists. The bifurcation of carried interest should be clearly stated. The bifurcation of carried interest should include the percentage of total carried interest to be paid to each of the general partners as well as the management company (fund economics Chapter 7). Many a time, carried interest is paid to venture capitalist after the LPs have gained their respective share of profit and sometimes carried interest paid to venture capitalist deal by deal. The deal by the deal payout of carried interest means that from every exit in the investee company, the profit will be distributed among the LPs, the general partners and the management company. The prospectus should include as to whichever way the VC firm wants to share the carried interest. The venture capitalists should also mention in the prospectus as to how carried interest was shared in previous funds, whether it be deal by deal or whole lump at the end of life of the fund. The VC firm should share distributed to a paid-in capital of each of the funds that the VC firm had run in the past.

An essential part of the fund-raising process is the inclusion of the total amount of capital the VC firm intends to raise for its next fund. The prospectus should include as to how much capital the VC firm intends to raise and out of this total amount how much capital is invested by general partners as well as the LPs. This information in prospectus reflects as to how much capital the general partners intend to invest and is one of the deciding factors among LPs whether to invest in a fund or not. If the general partners are investing handsome amount of capital (let's say more than 15% of total fund amount) in the fund then the LPs will be comfortable as deep inside they will think that there is too much capital of general partners at stake and so these general partners will not only take wise decisions regarding investments but also will manage portfolio companies in best possible manner.

As a part of fund intricacies, the prospectus should disclose as to how many companies the fund intends to invest in. The inclusion of too many companies in a portfolio can not only dilute the attention and focus but also deter the ability of management efficiently. In addition to the number of companies that will be included in the portfolio, the venture capitalist should also mention as to how much percentage on an average will be taken in each of the portfolio companies. Too much capital investment in a company also increases the amount of capital loss if the respective portfolio company fails to perform. The optimum amount of ownership should be taken in each of the portfolio companies to diversify the risk among stakeholders.

One of the most essential parts of the prospectus is the kind of industries that the venture capitalist will target while investing. Some industries are high in growth whereas some are slow or sluggish in growth. The high-growth industries yield relatively better returns if the portfolio companies achieve success. So, prospectus should cover why particular industry or industries will be targeted to identify, invest and build a portfolio of companies (as discussed in Chapter 4 on deal evaluation). Next part of fund intricacies includes as to which stage the fund will choose to invest while selecting portfolio companies. The stage can be pre-seed, seed, VC round A, round B or round C. Many a time, the venture capitalist intends to select a company based on industry, nature of product and team and the stage of the company does not matter. In such cases, it should be mentioned in the prospectus that portfolio companies will be selected irrespective of the stage of these companies.

Next part of fund intricacies includes the deal evaluation process. The venture capitalist should disclose the process that's followed to identify the portfolio companies (for deal evaluation process see Chapter 4). Lastly, the venture capitalist should make the projections regarding the performance of the fund and provided the anticipated return of the fund. The projections and anticipated return should be based on authentic and reliable assumptions.

To sum up the chapter of fund raising, the VC fund-raising process involves the building of prospectus and inviting investors to read prospectus and attend fund-raising campaigns of venture capitalists. The main ingredient of fund-raising process is prospectus of the fund. The prospectus should thoroughly cover the background as well as industry experience of the team of venture capitalists. Also, the prospectus should include fund intricacies and details as discussed above.

Bibliography

ABC Investments. 'Role of Venture Capital in the Economic Growth of the United States'. 2019. Available at: https://medium.com/@abc_40376/role-of-venture-capital-in-the-economic-growth-of-united-states–11b2090330a1 (accessed on 10 January 2020).

Abudheen, S. 'Yatra.com Raises $23M in a New Round from IDG Ventures and Temasek's VC Arm Vertex'. 2014. Available at: https://www.vccircle.com/yatracom-raises–23m-new-round-idg-ventures-and-temaseks-vc-arm-vertex/ (accessed on 28 October 2019).

Accel. 'Flipkart'. 2019. Available at: https://www.accel.com/companies/flipkart (accessed on 28 October 2019).

Alworth, Julian S., and Giampaolo Arachi. *Taxation and the Financial Crisis*. New York, NY: OUP Oxford, 2012.

Arsalidou, Demetra. *Rethinking Corporate Governance in Financial Institutions*. New York, NY: Routledge, 2015.

BerkeleyEconomics. 'TheEconomicsofIdeas: PaulRomer, formerBerkeley Economics Professor, Receives the 2018 Nobel Prize'. 2018. Available at: https://www.econ.berkeley.edu/content/guest-post-economist-ideas-paul-romer-former-berkeley-economics-professor-receives-2018 (accessed on 10 January 2020).

Bernstein, Shai, Xavier Giroud, and Richard R. Townsend. 'The Impact of Venture Capital Monitoring.' *The Journal of Finance* 71, no. 4 (2016): 1591–1622.

Bottazzi, Laura, Marco Da Rin, and Thomas Hellmann. 'The Importance of Trust for Investment: Evidence from Venture Capital.' *The Review of Financial Studies* 29, no. 9 (2016): 2283–2318.

Bragg, Steven M. *The New CFO Financial Leadership Manual*. Hoboken, NJ: John Wiley & Sons, 2011.

Camp, Justin J. *Venture Capital Due Diligence: A Guide to Making Smart Investment Choices and Increasing Your Portfolio Returns.* New York, NY: John Wiley & Sons, 2002.

Carver, Lorenzo. *Venture Capital Valuation: Case Studies and Methodology.* New Jersey, NJ: John Wiley & Sons, 2011.

Chanchani, M. 'Flipkart Investor Accel Raises $450 million for Fifth India Fund'. 2016. Available at: https://economictimes.indiatimes.com/small-biz/money/flipkart-investor-accel-raises−450-million-for-fifth-india-fund/articleshow/55706174.cms?from=mdr (accessed on 28 October 2019).

Chanchani, M. 'Nexus Venture Partners Eyes $400 million in Fifth Fund'. 2018. Available at: https://economictimes.indiatimes.com/small-biz/startups/newsbuzz/nexus-venture-partners-eyes−400-million-in-fifth-fund/articleshow/62598388.cms?from=mdr (accessed on 28 October 2019).

Chemmanur, Thomas J., Tyler J. Hull, and Karthik Krishnan. 'Do Local and International Venture Capitalists Play Well Together? The Complementarity of Local and International Venture Capitalists.' *Journal of Business Venturing* 31, no. 5 (2016): 573–594.

Chernenko, Sergey, Josh Lerner, and Yao Zeng. 'Mutual Funds as Venture Capitalists? Evidence from Unicorns'. NBER Working Paper No. w23981, National Bureau of Economic Research, USA, 2017.

Colombo, Massimo G., Douglas J. Cumming, and Silvio Vismara. 'Governmental Venture Capital for Innovative Young Firms.' *The Journal of Technology Transfer* 41, no. 1 (2016): 10–24.

Cremades, Alejandro. *The Art of Startup Fundraising: Pitching Investors, Negotiating the Deal, and Everything Else Entrepreneurs Need to Know.* New Jersey, NJ: John Wiley & Sons, 2016.

Cumming, Douglas, Irene Henriques, and Perry Sadorsky. '"Cleantech" Venture Capital Around the World.' *International Review of Financial Analysis* 44, (2016): 86–97.

Da Rin, M., and M. F. Penas. 'The Effect of Venture Capital on Innovation Strategies'. NBER Working Paper No. w13636, 2007. Available at SSRN: http://ssrn.com/abstract=1033761.

Damodaran, Aswath. *Investment Valuation: Tools and Techniques for Determining the Value of Any Asset*. Hoboken, NJ: Wiley Finance, 2012.

Demaria, Cyril. *Introduction to Private Equity: Venture, Growth, LBO and Turn-Around Capital*. West Sussex: John Wiley & Sons, 2010.

ET Bureau. 'Is the Job Scene in India Bad? Depends on How You See It, Says Govt'. 2019. Available at: https://economictimes. indiatimes.com/jobs/indias-unemployment-rate-hit-6-1-in-2017-18/ articleshow/69598640.cms?from=mdr (accessed on 10 January 2020).

Feld, Brad, and Jason Mendelson. *Venture Deals: Be Smarter Than Your Lawyer and Venture Capitalist*. Danvers, MA: John Wiley & Sons, 2011.

Gadiesh, O., and H. MacArthur. *Lessons from Private Equity Any Company Can Use (Memo to the CEO)*. Brighton, MA: Harvard Business Publishing, 2008.

Gerken, Louis C., and W. A. Whittaker. *The Little Book of Venture Capital Investing: Empowering Economic Growth and Investment Portfolios*. Hoboken, NJ: John Wiley & Sons, 2014.

Geroski, P. Gilbert, and A. Jacquemin. *Barriers to Entry and Strategic Competition*. London: Routledge, 1990.

Gibbons, Gary, Robert D. Hisrich, and Carlos M. DaSilva. 2014. *Entrepreneurial Finance: A Global Perspective*. Thousand Oaks, CA: SAGE Publications.

Golis, Christopher C. *Enterprise and Venture Capital: A Business Builder's and Investor's Handbook*. Crows West: Allen & Unwin, 2002.

Gompers, Paul A., Will Gornall, Steven N. Kaplan, and Ilya A. Strebulaev. 'How do venture capitalists make decisions?' *Journal of Financial Economics* 135, no. 1 (2019): 169–190.

Gooptu, B. 'Policybazaar Raises $5 million from Inventus Capital, Info Edge and Intel Capital'. 2013. Available at: https://economictimes.indiatimes.com/industry/banking/finance/policybazaar-raises–5-million-from-inventus-capital-info-edge-and-intel-capital/articleshow/19441695.cms?from=mdr (accessed on 28 October 2019).

Green, Milford B. *Venture Capital: International Comparisons*. Oxon: Routledge, 1991.

Gregoriou, Greg N. *Encyclopedia of Alternative Investments*. Boca Raton, FL: CRC Press, 2008.

Haislip, Alexander. *Essentials of Venture Capital*. Hoboken, NJ: John Wiley & Sons, 2010.

Hellmann, Thomas, Paul Schure, and Dan Vo. 'Angels and Venture Capitalists: Complements or Substitutes?' Finance Working Paper No. 628, European Corporate Governance Institute—Finance, 2019. Available at SSRN: https://ssrn.com/abstract=2602739 or http://dx.doi.org/10.2139/ssrn.2602739

Hisrich, Robert D., Saša Petković, Veland Ramadani, and Léo-Paul Dana. 'Venture Capital Funds in Transition Countries: Insights from Bosnia and Herzegovina and Macedonia.' *Journal of Small Business and Enterprise Development* 23, no. 2 (2016): 296–315.

IHS Global Insight, *Venture Impact: The Economic Impact of Venture Capital-Backed Companies to the US Economy*. A Report Prepared for National Venture Capital Association, 2009. Available at: http://faculty.msmc.edu/hossain/grad_bank_and_money_policy/economic%20importance%20of%20venture%20capital%20backed%20companies.pdf (accessed on 1 May 2020).

Inc42. 'Top 47 Most Active Venture Capital Firms In India For Startups'. 2019. Available at: https://inc42.com/resources/top-47-active-venture-capital-firms-india-startups/ (accessed on 28 October 2019).

Khurshed, Arif. *Initial Public Offerings: The Mechanics and Performance of IPOs*. Petersfield: Harriman House Limited, 2011.

KJ, S. 'Sequoia Capital Sheds Further 5% Stake in JustDial for ₹135 Crore' (2017). Available at: https://www.medianama.com/2017/09/223-sequoia-capital-sheds-further-5-stake-in-justdial-for-rs-135-crore/ (accessed on 28 October 2019).

Klausner, Michael, and Kate Litvak. 'What Economists Have Taught Us About Venture Capital Contracting'. In *Bridging the Entrepreneurial Financing Gap*, edited by Michael J. Whincop, 54–74. London: Routledge, 2017.

Klonowski, Darek. *The Venture Capital Investment Process*. New York, NY: Springer, 2010.

Kumar, S. 'PolicyBazaar—Story, Founder, Business Model, Funding, Team, News'. 2019. Available at: https://startuptalky.com/startup-story-policy-bazaar/ (accessed on 28 October 2019).

Kupor, Scott. *Secrets of Sand Hill Road: Venture Capital and How to Get It*. London: Penguin Publishing Group, 2019.

Lockett, A., M. Wright, A. Burrows, L. Scholes, and D. Paton. 'The Export Intensity of Venture Capital-backed Companies.' *Small Business Economics: An Entrepreneurship Journal* 31, no. 1 (2008): 39–58.

Malmström, Malin, Jeaneth Johansson, and Joakim Wincent. 'Gender Stereotypes and Venture Support Decisions: How Governmental Venture Capitalists Socially Construct Entrepreneurs' Potential.' *Entrepreneurship Theory and Practice* 41, no. 5 (2017): 833–860.

Manigart, Sophie, and Harry Sapienza, 'Venture Capital and Growth,' in *The Blackwell Handbook of Entrepreneurship*, edited by Donald L. Sexton and Hans Landström, 240–258. Oxford: Blackwell Publisher, 1999.

Markides, Constantinos C., and Paul A. Geroski. *Fast Second: How Smart Companies Bypass Radical Innovation to Enter and Dominate New Markets*. San Francisco, SF: John Wiley & Sons, 2004.

Mason, C. M., and R. T. Harrison. 'Improving Access to Early Stage Venture Capital in Regional Economies: A New Approach to Investment Readiness', *Local Economy* 19, no. 2 (2004): 159–173.

Mishra, R. K., and T. Satyanarayana Chary. *Venture Capital Financing for Biotechnology*. New Delhi: Concept Publishing Company, 2008.

Mollick, Ethan, and Alicia Robb. 'Democratizing Innovation and Capital Access: The Role of Crowdfunding.' *California Management Review* 58, no. 2 (2016): 72–87.

Parhankangas, A. (n.d.), 'The Economic Impact of Venture Capital'. In *Handbook of Research on Venture Capital: Volume 2*, edited by Hans Landström & Colin Mason, 124–158. Cheltenham: Edward Elgar Publishing, 2012.

Pearce, Rupert, and Simon Barnes. *Raising Venture Capital*. West Sussex: John Wiley & Sons, 2006.

Policybazaar.com. 'Our Investors'. 2019. Available at: https://www.policybazaar.com/investors/ (accessed on 28 October 2019).

Povaly, Stefan. *Private Equity Exits: Divestment Process Management for Leveraged Buyouts*. Berlin: Springer Science & Business Media, 2007.

Samila, Sampsa, and Olav Sorenson. 'Venture Capital, Entrepreneurship, and Economic Growth.' *Review of Economics and Statistics* 93, no. 1 (2011): 338–349.

Schell, James M. *Private Equity Funds: Business Structure and Operations*. New York, NY: Law Journal Press, 2018.

Senor, D., and Singer, S. *Start-up Nation: The Story of Israel's Economic Miracle*. New York, NY: Hachette Book Group, 2009.

Sirkin, Michael S., and Lawrence K. Cagney. *Executive Compensation*. New York, NY: Law Journal Press, 2018.

Stefanova, Mariya. *Private Equity Accounting, Investor Reporting, and Beyond: Advanced Guide for Private Equity Managers, Institutional Investors, Investment Professionals, and Students*. Upper Saddle River, NJ: FT Press, 2015.

Stowell, David P. *An Introduction to Investment Banks, Hedge Funds, and Private Equity*. London: Academic Press, 2010.

Susmit, S. 'Sequoia Capital Sells Just Dial Stake Worth ₹51.56 crore'. 2017. Available at: https://www.livemint.com/Companies/biwDbxNR1yxIehl935GsuN/Sequoia-Capital-sells-Just-Dial-stake-worth-Rs5156-crore.html (accessed on 28 October 2019).

Ueda, M., and M. Hirukawa. 'Venture Capital and Productivity.' CEPR Discussion Paper No. DP7089, University of Wisconsin, Madison, USA, 2003. Available at: https://ssrn.com/abstract=1344668 (accessed on 1 May 2020).

Vries, Harm F. de, Menno J. van Loon, and Sjoerd Mol. 2016. *Venture Capital Deal Terms: A Guide to Negotiating and Structuring Venture Capital Transactions.* Pumbo.nl B.V.

Wallmeroth, Johannes, Peter Wirtz, and Alexander Peter Groh. 'Venture Capital, Angel Financing, and Crowdfunding of Entrepreneurial Ventures: A Literature Review.' *Foundations and Trends® in Entrepreneurship* 14, no. 1 (2018): 1–129.

Wasserman, Noam. *The Founder's Dilemmas: Anticipating and Avoiding the Pitfalls That Can Sink a Startup.* Oxfordshire: Princeton University Press, 2013.

Zi-yao, X. U. 'Do Corporate Venture Capitalists Add Value to Start-up Firms.' *Economic Theory and Business Management* 4 (2016): 4.

About the Authors

Raj Kumar is a distinguished academician, researcher and educational administrator. He is currently the Vice Chancellor of Panjab University, Chandigarh. He completed his PhD from Banaras Hindu University (BHU) and DLitt from University of Lucknow. He brings with him a rich mixture of professional integrity and administrative experience. Professor Raj Kumar has been actively engaged in teaching, research, training and consultancy in management field for more than three decades. He has been Director, Dean and Head of Institute of Management Studies, BHU, Varanasi.

Professor Raj Kumar has mentored more than a dozen PhD students, published many books and more than a hundred research papers in the journals of national and international repute. He has been on the editorial board of more than two dozen international and national journals such as *American Journal of Industrial and Business Management*, *International Journal of Advanced Scientific Research and Development*, *BHU Management Review*, *Finance India*, etc.

He is a chairman of various decision-making bodies of most prestigious institutions such as Post Graduate Institute of Medical Education and Research (PGIMER); State Higher Education Council, RUSA; Chandigarh Region Innovation and Knowledge Cluster (CRIKC); Regional Advisory Committee of Kendriya Vidyalaya Sangathan; Standing Committee for SC/ST; UGC-SAP; and UGC–CAS II of different departments of Panjab University.

SAGE ESSENTIALS

He is the member of Indian Institute of Public Administration (IIPA), New Delhi; Administrator's Advisory Council, Chandigarh; Punjab State Council for Science & Technology; the governing body of the Inter-University Centre for Astronomy and Astrophysics (IUCAA), Pune; Board of Governors of Punjab Engineering College, Chandigarh; academic council of various universities and chairman of a number of UGC expert committees.

Manu Sharma is assistant professor in University Institute of Applied Management Sciences, Panjab University. He is a PhD in Finance from Swiss Management Centre University, Switzerland, and has done his MBA (Finance) from University of Massa-chusetts, Boston, Massachusetts. Prior to this, he worked with ICICI Bank as Manager in SME financing sector and GE Capital International Services, USA, as Assistant Manager for Capital Markets Group. He has also worked with Trudeau & Trudeau Associates, USA, as Valuation Consultant-Investment Banking.

Apart from teaching, Dr Sharma works as consultant with Providence Solutions Pvt Ltd and works on writing business plans as well as raising private equity for high-growth companies. He works on performing valuations of companies for the purpose of private equity investments as well as for mergers and acquisitions. He has published extensively in *Journal of Private Equity* (Institutional Investors, New York) and has even created an 'Asset Pricing' theory to value 'Venture Capital Investments' (published in November 2015, *Journal of Private Equity*, USA). He has written books on mergers and acquisitions and financial derivatives that have been prescribed in institutions such as S. P. Jain Institute of Management and Research and Institute of Management Technology (IMT) Ghaziabad.